MW01122285

2009 09 21

The *Masks* of *Judith Thompson*

The Masks
of
Judith Thompson

Edited by Ric Knowles

Playwrights Canada Press
Toronto • Canada

Playwrights Canada Press
215 Spadina Avenue, Suite 230, Toronto, Ontario CANADA M5T 2C7
416-703-0013   fax 416-408-3402
orders@playwrightscanada.com • www.playwrightscanada.com

Financial support provided by the taxpayers of Canada and Ontario through the Canada
Council for the Arts and the Department of Canadian Heritage through the Book Publishing
Industry Development Programme, and the Ontario Arts Council.

Cover photo of Judith Thompson by Dean Palmer
Production Editor/Cover Design: JLArt

Library and Archives Canada Cataloguing in Publication

The masks of Judith Thompson / edited by Ric Knowles.

Includes bibliographical references.
ISBN 0-88754-900-4

1. Thompson, Judith, 1954- --Criticism and interpretation.
I. Knowles, Ric

PS8589.H4883Z76 2006   C812'.54   C2006-902366-2

First edition: May 2006
Printed and bound by Hignell Printing at Winnipeg, Canada.

To Christine

❖

Table of Contents

❖

Acknowledgements

This volume is entirely dependent on the support of Angela Rebeiro, who was behind it from the outset, and who commissioned the volume as one of her last acts as Publisher of Playwrights Canada Press before her much lamented retirement. It also relies on the work of Jodi Armstrong, who as always has been brilliant, consultative, and hugely supportive, and on the research assistance of Corrie Hodgson, Gord Lester, and Amanda McCoy. And of course it rests entirely on the words and work of my colleague, the remarkable Judith Thompson.

Nigel Hunt's "In Contact with the Dark" was first published in *Books in Canada* 17.2 (March 1988): 10-12; Sandra Tomc's "Revisions of Probability: An Interview with Judith Thompson" was first published in *Canadian Theatre Review* 59 (Summer 1989): 18-23; Cynthia Zimmerman's "A Conversation with Judith Thompson" was first published in *Canadian Drama/L'Art dramatique canadien* 16.2 (1990), 184-94; Judith Thompson's "One Twelfth" was first published in *Language in Her Eye: Visions on Writing Gender by Canadian Women Writing in English*, ed. Libby Scheier, Sarah Sheard, and Eleanor Wachtel (Toronto: Coach House, 1990, 263-67); Judith Rudakoff's "Judith Thompson: Interview" was first published in *Fair Play: 12 Women Speak (Conversations with Canadian Playwrights)*, ed. Judith Rudakoff and Rita Much (Toronto: Simon & Pierre, 1990, 8-104); Eleanor Wachtel's "An Interview with Judith Thompson" was first published in *Brick: A Journal of Reviews* 41 (Summer 1991), 37-41; "Offending your Audience" (Panel Discussion), from which I have excerpted here, was first published in *Theatrum* 29 (June/July/August 1992), 33-34; Judith Thompson's "Why Should a Playwright Direct Her Own Plays?" was first published in *Women on the Canadian Stage: The Legacy of Hrotsvit*, ed. Rita Much (Winnipeg: Blizzard, 1992), 104-08); Ric Knowles's "Computers Keep Your Office Tidier" was first published in *Canadian Theatre Review* 81 (Winter 1994), 29-31; Judith Thompson's "No Soy Culpable" was first published in *Writing Away: The PEN Canada Travel Anthology*, ed. Constance Rooke (Toronto: McClelland and Stewart, 1994), 307-16; Judith Thompson's "Mouthful of Pearls" was first published in *The Monkey and Other Stories*, ed. Griffin Ondaatje (Toronto: Harper Collins, 1995), 209-17; Soraya Peerbaye's "Look to the Lady: Re-examining Women's Theatre (Six Women in a Roundtable Discussion)," from which I have excerpted here, was first published in *Canadian Theatre Review* 81 (Fall 1995), 22-25; Judith Thompson's "Second Thoughts (What I'd Be If I Were Not A Writer)" was first published in *Brick* 51 (Winter 1995), 26-29; Judith Thompson's "Epilepsy & the Snake: Fear in the Creative Process" was first published in *Canadian Theatre Review* 89 (Winter

1996), 4-7; Jennifer Fletcher's "The Last Things in the Sled: An Interview with Judith Thompson" was first published in *Canadian Theatre Review* 89 (Winter 1996), 39-41; Andrew Vowles's "Inside Playwright Judith Thompson: Behind the Mask" was first published in *Guelph Alumnus: The University of Guelph Magazine* (Winter 1999), 20-25; "Turning an Elephant into a Microphone: A Conversation on Translation and Adaptation," ed. Ric Knowles, from which I have excerpted here, was first published in *Canadian Theatre Review* 114 (Spring 2003), 47-53; Judith Thompson's "'I Will Tear You to Pieces': The Classroom as Theatre" was first published in *How Theatre Educates: Convergences and Counterpoints With Artists, Scholars and Advocates*, ed. Kathleen Gallagher and David Booth (Toronto: U of Toronto P, 2003), 25-34; Judith Thompson's "'It's My Birthday Forever Now': Urjo Kareda and Me" was first published in *Canadian Theatre Review* 113 (Winter 2003), 11-14; Robyn Read's "Witnessing the Workshop Process of Judith Thompson's *Capture Me*: Mothers, Masks and Monsters: A Conversation Between Teacher and Student" was first published in *Canadian Theatre Review* 120 (Fall 2004), 96-100; Judith Thompson's "Beyond the U.S.A., Beyond the U.K.: A View from Canada" was first published in *Women Writing Plays: Three Decades of the Susan Smith Blackburn Prize*, ed. Alexis Greene (Austin: U of Texas P), 2006. Ann Holloway's "Hedda & Lynndie & Jabber & Ciel" was commissioned for this volume and is published here for the first time. The cover image of Judith Thompson was taken by Dean Palmer, and first appeared in *Guelph Alumnus: The University of Guelph Magazine* (Winter 1999), 20. Everything in this volume is published with the permission of the copyright holder.

Introduction:
"Warts and Zigzags:" The Masks of Judith Thompson
by Ric Knowles

The story of Judith Thompson's coming to writing through a mask class at the National Theatre School of Canada is well known. It is told on the first page of the first article in this volume, based on Thompson's earliest extended interview, and it has been retold frequently since. But masks are much more than the route through which Thompson discovered herself as a writer. They are her *way* of writing, as she turns her back on her own public persona and dons the masks of each of her characters in order to discover what they have to say and their richly various ways of saying it. Masks are also her central technique as a teacher of both acting and playwriting, as she brings her students to an understanding of themselves and a discovery of their voices by having them inhabit the psyches and voices of others. And they are also, I suggest, her mode of self-presentation in interviews and writings about her own work. "I should make something up," as she says to interviewer Nigel Hunt. And in writing about her background, process, and ways of working she will often use the third-person "Judith," or "she" rather than the autobiographical "I," to at once protect and free herself.

As you approach this book of interviews, contributions to panels, and writings in which Judith Thompson discusses her own work, then, its cover image by photographer Dean Palmer, showing her with her back to the camera but foregrounding a theatrical mask, issues a *caveat lector*. You will find in this volume several brilliant and honest performances as Judith dons her various masks, presenting herself in the different roles writer, actor, director, teacher, mother, "girl," (un)feminist, passionate advocate, packrat of other people's stories, and "*idiot savant*" (as she often calls herself in her early interviews). She even dons what Judith Rudakoff here calls "the civilized mask." You will find many links among the roles, and many insights into her writing. You will not find "the essential Judith," but you may encounter some of the "eleven other Judiths" that she herself sets out to recover in her essays "One Twelfth" and "Epilepsy & the Snake."

The Masks of Judith Thompson is intended as a companion volume to *Judith Thompson*, a collection of critical essays published in 2005 by Playwrights Canada Press. The introduction and contents of that book surveyed the history of Judith Thompson's work in scholarly criticism from the appearance in 1988 of the first major article on her plays to new material published there for the first time. This volume takes a similar shape—from the earliest full-length interview article by Nigel Hunt, first published in *Books in Canada* in 1988, to a newly commissioned interview by Ann Holloway, published here for the first time. But in this book, Thompson herself has control of the discourse.

Over her career, Judith Thompson has been the subject of many interviews, has taken part in many panel discussions, and has been invited to contribute writings about her work to a wide variety of publications. A selection of these interviews, published panels, and writings is presented here in the order in which they first appeared—many of them in sources that are now difficult to find. These pieces range widely in genre from the autobiographical through the expository to the fictional, and they cover issues that range from biographical matters of family, education, monsters, snakes, fear, dreams, pregnancy, health, seizure disorder, and Catholicism; through social issues such as gender, class, psychology, and politics; to questions about her creative inspiration in daily life, such as newspaper stories, her students, her family, her dreams (again), "nail soup," "chaos," and her own psyche; and finally to dramaturgical issues about form, style, language, process, and method. These writings and discussions read intriguingly against the plays, screenplays, radio dramas and adaptations that they complement and illuminate, but apart from the key early interviews by Sandra Tomc, Cynthia Zimmerman, and Judith Rudakoff reprinted here, they have rarely been drawn upon in critical discussions of Thompson's work.

Thompson's own non-dramatic writings cover considerable ground. The earliest piece about her work published here, "One Twelfth," written in 1990 for a collection by women writers about writing as a woman, addresses an issue that comes up repeatedly in this volume: Thompson's relationship to feminism, in her life and in her writing. She first calls the autobiographical mask in this essay an "unfeminist feminist," but a few paragraphs later "she" is "a feminist" *tout court*. And equally paradoxically, Thompson engages throughout the essay in an acute feminist self-analysis concerning her own personal struggles and failures *as* a feminist writer, mother, partner, and citizen. Thompson also circles around what for her is the vexed issue of feminism in her 1989 interview with Sandra Tomc, where she identifies as feminist but offers stern criticism of what she understands to be strands of feminist thought that might limit the universality of her undertaking, constrain the breadth of her representations of women, or restrict her representation of the "Truth," as she says most explicitly in her 1990 interview with Judith Rudakoff. Nevertheless, in the story "Mouthful of Pearls," in her trenchant comments on the gendering of the theatre in the panel "Look to the Lady"—where she discusses having learned early in life to don the "mask of a girl" made for her by men—and elsewhere, she exhibits an acute, lived awareness of the operations of patriarchy. And in her most recent article about her own work, "Beyond the U.S.A., Beyond the U.K.," published in 2006 almost simultaneously with this volume, in the Susan Smith Blackburn Prize anthology, Thompson returns to the topic of her feminist sensibility, which she describes as emerging along with her Canadian nationalism and her voice as a playwright, through the liberating assumption of an ungendered, neutral mask.

Similarly complex is Thompson's relationship to issues of class. In her early interviews she distances herself from her (somewhat caricatured) "Marxists friends" (Rudakoff)—I fear I may have been one of them—and insists on the universality of the humanity that she represents. "My characters don't have a social group," she insists in her interview with Judith Rudakoff, and later says "It doesn't matter what class the man is from," when asked about Joe in *The Crackwalker*. She says similar things in her interview with Eleanor Wachtel—"it wasn't about the class thing so much as about these human beings." But two years earlier she had told Sandra Tomc that class is "pretty important" to her, and eight years later she tells Andrew Vowles that "a lot of my work is about class, about the class differentiation in Canada." Indeed, any careful reading of the plays will notice her unique sensitivity to class distinctions as marked by language, confidence, and naturalized social power, to the degree that class forms much of the social fabric and subject of the plays.

When I was preparing this volume I realized how active Thompson had been in the year or so up to its press deadline, and wanted to make sure that the book kept pace with her astonishing and ongoing career—picking up energy rather than declining after twenty-five active and celebrated years. So I asked her if she would be willing to be interviewed again before the book went to press, as a way of "covering" some of her newest material while still tracing the trajectory of her career. She immediately replied that yes, she would be happy to be interviewed:

> I would really like to have the chance to do a fresh interview. Sometimes people bring up things I have said in the past that I no longer believe at all—and, sometimes, didn't at the time, but was taken out of context... e.g. "I am not a feminist writer." Or the really famous one, "good lines are a dime a dozen." Well, that's true in the sense that sometimes we have to be willing to throw away lines to make the machine of the play move; on the other hand, when too much is sacrificed to the machine, one can lose the warts and zigzags that make the piece unique. Sometimes one can lose the very essence of the piece.

The response is characteristically frank, revisionist, and generous, and the result of that exchange is an interview with Thompson's long-time friend and collaborator (as an actor) Ann Holloway that is published here for the first time. The interview doesn't, in fact, revisit her previous interviews. Typically, she moves on. In fact the interview explores and exposes the extraordinary spectrum of Thompson's reach and range of sympathies in her most recent work, from the "classical" character and demeanor of the aristocratic but sexually repressed Hedda Gabler (as revisited by Thompson-as-adaptor in her two versions of Ibsen's play), through the abject but (in)famous "white-trash" sensibility, sensitively if shockingly re-imagined in her version of Private Lynndie England of the U.S. army in *My Pyramids, or How I Got Fired From The Dairy Queen and Ended Up at Abu Ghraib, by Pvt. Lynndie England,* to the obscurity of the mentally challenged and societally marginalized Parkdale residents, Jabber and Ciel in *Enoch Arden, by Alfred Lord Jabber and His Catatonic Songstress.* The interview suggests that the distance from Gabler to Jabber, in work written over so compressed a time period, is not so great after all—not, at least, for Judith Thompson. It also suggests that her writing career has returned her to subjects not dissimilar—except in style— from those of *The Crackwalker,* about the marginalized human underbelly of Kingston, Ontario.

But as she herself says in her comment to Andrew Vowles, Thompson's work has always moved, if often jarringly, between classes, between the Hedda Gablers of this world and its Lövbergs, between Lomia and Pony in *White Biting Dog,* Dee and Toilane in *I Am Yours,* Francesca and Patsy in *Perfect Pie,* Annie and Kevin in *Sled,* and Margaret and Lewis in *Habitat*—even between Lucy and Nellie in the short but powerful monologue "Pink," where the central issue is as much about class as race. Indeed, it may be less that humanity in her work is universal than that she explores the consistency and familiarity of class and power differentials and the conflicts that they produce.

In her early interviews Thompson frequently states that her work is not explicitly or narrowly political ("to be political is to bend the Truth," as she tells Judith Rudakoff), but a work such as *Sled,* when read against Thompson's comments on immigration in her interview with Jennifer Fletcher and in "No Soy Culpable," suggests a clear and direct politic. The same is even more true of *Habitat,* Thompson's only real "issue play" to date, in which she savvily confronted the largely suburban middle class CanStage audience at its first production with the Not-In-My-Back-Yard syndrome. The play resonates directly with her many comments on middle-class complacency, including her own, throughout this volume. Even *Capture Me* can be read together with Thompson's interview with Robyn Read as emerging from an explicitly political stance on immigration, racism, and violence against women. And of course *My Pyramids* directly takes on contemporary political events in the U.S. and the world; although it focuses its attention on one woman and her media demonization, it is also directly political in a larger sense, as Thompson's interview with Ann Holloway makes clear. But as she had said to Cynthia Zimmerman fifteen years earlier, "it's not at all about a particular platform. You have to change your whole sense of who you are in the world."

The second piece of writing by Thompson in this volume, first published in 1992, addresses professional issues, though ironically it also presents one of her most acute gender (and postcolonial) critiques. Here she writes about the relationship between playwright and director—female playwright and male director—first touched on in her 1990 interviews with Cynthia Zimmerman and Judith Rudakoff, and asks "Why Should a Playwright Direct Her Own Play?" The essay introduces the subject of the sometimes fraught relationships between Thompson and her collaborators that is another theme running throughout this book. The question comes up in comments made by Bill Glassco, the director of *White Biting Dog*, in the essay by Nigel Hunt that opens this volume, and Thompson herself addresses it there and in a number of other interviews as an issue of control, knowledge, and of ownership of the plays—at least as they are shaped in their premieres. Nigel Hunt and Andrew Vowles both quote the frequently-cited direction that prefaces the published script of *White Biting Dog*, suggesting the playwright's desire to control decisions that are usually left to actors and directors:

> Because of the extreme and deliberate musicality of this play, any attempts to go against the textual rhythms, such as the breaking up of an unbroken sentence, the taking of a pause where none is written in, are DISASTROUS.

But a picture emerges throughout this book, too, of a certain creative volatility in Thompson's way of working that has had an impact on her relationships with directors, actors, and, heartbreakingly, even her long-time mentor and dramaturg, Urjo Kareda, as she describes in her confessional piece, "It's My Birthday Forever Now." And a similar creative volatility seems also to be the engine that drives much of Thompson's classroom practice, as is clear from her extraordinary account of it in "'I Will Tear You to Pieces': The Classroom as Theatre," an essay written in 2003 for a collection of essays on *How Theatre Educates*. Further insight into her teaching and its relationship to her writing emerges from Vowles' profile, and of course from Robyn Read's 2004 "Conversation Between Teacher and Student," where Read acutely notes the link between Thompson's pedagogical practice and the central settings, characters, and subject matter of *Capture Me*.

But Thompson has not only caused offence on occasion to her collaborators and students in the creative hothouses that can be her rehearsal halls and classrooms; she has also been accused of "Offending [the] Audience," as the title of one panel indicates. She finds this both surprising and inevitable in a society founded, as she says, on denial ("Offending"), but as her 1991 interview with Eleanor Wachtel suggests, it also has to do with her attraction to the dark side of the psyche, to the hidden, to the disturbing. In any Judith Thompson play the stakes are high and the situations uncomfortable. As Andrew Vowles' leading question suggests, the plays are "dark, disturbing, full of angry people, full of profanity…," and they can often confront complacency with its own complicity in the creation or exploitation of what it doesn't want to know. But as Wachtel's urging of the issue also suggests, the plays can walk a fine line between exploitation and giving voice—a line that Thompson walks as no other Canadian playwright has succeeded in doing. And as several interviews reveal, the cost of walking that line is high for the playwright as well. "Second Thoughts (What I'd Be If I Were Not a Writer)," is a revealing autobiographical piece that suggests the stakes involved for Judith Thompson in being a writer, as opposed to the plant-watering, peaceful employment for which she sometimes longs.

Elsewhere in this volume Thompson provides many other insights, large and small, into her creative and rehearsal processes, in interviews, papers, and panels about the sources of her inspiration (Hunt, Zimmerman, Rudakoff, "Epilepsy"), about her teachers and mentors ("Beyond," "It's My Birthday"), about her workshop and revision processes (Fletcher, Read, Vowles), about her gravitational pull towards the naturalistic style (Fletcher), about donning the neutral mask of the translator ("Turning an Elephant into a Microphone"), and even about such mundane things as her use of computers to keep her office tidier, in an interview first published in an issue of *Canadian Theatre Review* on "Computing Theatre" (Knowles).

Seemingly anomalous in this collection is "No Soy Culpable," written for PEN Canada's *Writing Away* collection in 1994. But the piece is revealing of Thompson's sensibility: her curiosity ("I am hungry for the unfamiliar"), her shame at encounters with Mexican poverty and courage that challenge middle-class Canadian comforts, her contradictions, and her Canadian-ness, which never leaves her, even when she leaves Canada. Also seemingly anomalous here is the dialogue story, "Mouthful of Pearls," included in spite of its being a piece of creative fiction, because it is little known and yet has so many suggestive parallels to Thompson's dramatic work, particularly works such as *Lion in the Streets*, *Capture Me*, and especially the short play, "A Kissing Way," that deal with sexual violence.

Finally, of course, the articles, interviews, and panels published here provide insight into individual plays, and reading them against the plays that she was writing at their various times of first publication provides flashes of insight that can light up dark corners of the work. Eleanor Wachtel's probing into the optimistic ending of as bleak a play as *Lion in the Streets* comes to mind, as do Sandra Tomc's inquiries about the relationships between Dee's experiences of pregnancy in *I Am Yours* and Thompson's own. But perhaps the most useful interviews in this regard are those on *Sled* and *Capture Me* with her student assistants Jennifer Fletcher and Robyn Read, and on *Hedda Gabler*, *Enoch Arden* and *My Pyramids* with Ann Holloway, where the opportunity to speak at length on specific works provides an expansiveness that will be useful to anyone interested in these remarkable plays. Jennifer Fletcher's interview draws essential attention, for students of *Sled*, to the so-called "Barbecue Dream Scene," a scene that Thompson argues is central to an informed understanding of the play, but one that is not included in the published script, having been cut during the workshop process.[1] The interview also explicates specific passages, such as Kevin's "Northern Lights" speech, in ways that are gifts to students and researchers. Read's interview is similarly suggestive for students of *Capture Me*—particularly for understanding the difficult characters of Dodge, Aziz, Delphine, and of course Jerry herself, whose final sacrifice is deeply troubling, particularly to feminist spectators. And the final interview in the volume, with Ann Holloway, herself an actor who has performed in several Judith Thompson productions, brings to the reader a sense of what the three shows they discuss felt like in the theatre. It also brings out Thompson's own readings—such as her certainty that Hedda Gabler was abused by her father—that inevitably leave traces in the work that might otherwise be inscrutable.

But much about Judith Thompson remains inscrutable, masked. This volume neither attempts nor could wish to reveal what lies behind the mask, except, of course, for another mask, and then another. For Thompson, the masks that she dons as a writer, actor, teacher, and interview subject are enabling. Like the neutral mask given to her twenty-five years ago by Pierre Lefevre at National Theatre School, the mask that freed her voice, led to the creation of her first and most famous play, and "changed [her] life" ("Beyond"), these masks are liberating, life-affirming. They are the source of her politics, her craft, her power, and her "Truth."

Note

[1] The scene is published in Ric Knowles's "'Great Lines Are a Dime a Dozen': Judith Thompson's Greatest Cuts," *Canadian Theatre Review* 89 (Winter 1996): 8-18.

In Contact with the Dark
by Nigel Hunt

Judith Thompson seems embarrassed—sorry to disappoint anyone with dull personal details that cannot hope to compete with the intensity and eccentricity of what she writes for the stage. She apologizes, "This is going to bore everybody to death." Then her writer's imagination jumps into gear and she smiles, having thought of a better story than the mere mundane truth. Her eyes narrow, she brushes back her long brown hair and leans forward slightly. "I should make something up. I was a clown in a circus…"

For a new playwright, Judith Thompson is very well known. Her work has won her great attention and respect over a professional career of only eight years. Born in Montreal in 1954, she graduated from Queen's University in Kingston in 1976. She then went to the National Theatre School to train for an acting career. In mask class, the students were asked to come up with monologues for their characters. "I really ignited there," says Thompson. Improvisation class excited her, too. She quickly turned the stimulation of these acting exercises into the foundation of her first play: "I started turning a monologue into a scene and a scene into another scene. And I thought, 'Well, we should have some guys enter. We should have a little conflict.' And then it turned into *The Crackwalker*."

The Crackwalker is a frighteningly realistic look at the underbelly of our society. It relates the painful and pathetic life of a retarded woman, Theresa, and her friends, all of whom try and fail to fit into a life-style that lies forever beyond their grasp. While the play communicates a strong sense of their sordid desolation, it also never fails to evoke their warmth and humour. If Theresa's life "sucking off queers down the Lido for five bucks," is depressing and her utter failure to mother her retarded baby repellent, we still feel for Thompson's characters' painful need to love, and their inability to do so—a recurring theme in all Thompson's plays. A drunk vomits on a man's shoes. Theresa enters with her dead baby in a shopping bag. Sandy tells Theresa, "I get off on cornbeef on rye, arsewipe, why d'ya think I need the fuckin' money." Alan cracks an egg over his head in frustration from losing his job, confessing, "Did you ever start thinkin' somethin', and it's like, ugly…? And ya can't beat it out of your head?" Joe and Theresa are both compulsively unfaithful to their spouses. Theresa fantasizes that "I look like the Virgin and she hardly pretty… Hey, beebee, if I lookin' like her and she holdin' beebee Jesus like I holdin' you, you mus' look like Jesus!" Thompson does not betray the reality of her characters by imposing change on their lives. At the play's end, we leave them as we found them. The change the playwright wishes to effect is in her audience; not in her characters.

Thompson's first play brought her public recognition, but she insists that its reputation as an instant hit is simply a myth. *The Crackwalker* was a finalist in both the Clifford E. Lee playwrights' competition and the National Repertory Theatre Play Awards in 1980; the play opened that November at Theatre Passe Muraille in a production directed by Clarke Rogers. The initial reviews were not favourable. As Thompson, recalls, shaking her head, "Gina Mallet hated it." The play was picked up by the Centaur Theatre in Montreal two years later, and it was there that *The Crackwalker* found an audience and critical acclaim; the *Gazette* called the play an "exquisite provocation." Audiences flocked to see it, and *The Crackwalker* returned to Toronto where, as Thompson puts it, the critics "all rode on the bandwagon and wrote good reviews." *The Globe and Mail*'s Ray Conlogue praised Thompson's "remorseless honesty," and, despite the play's "gutter language," even the *Toronto Sun*'s usually reserved Bob Pennington conceded, "Rarely can a standing ovation in our alternative theatre have been more thoroughly deserved."

Thompson's second play, *White Biting Dog*, premiered at Tarragon Theatre in 1984 and won that year's Governor General's Award for drama; it has since been produced in Chicago and Vancouver, among other places. Winning this award was important for Thompson. It compensated for some of the nasty reviews that the play had received: "It's like a child that's been mistreated—you feel vindicated," the playwright says. Her latest play, *I Am Yours*, was also produced at the Tarragon Theatre and was chosen as a runner-up in the 1987 Floyd S. Chalmers Canadian Play Awards in January. Thompson has also written several scripts for CBC radio, television, and film.

I Am Yours tells the story of a woman named Dee, who wreaks havoc in the lives of two men to whom she is attracted. Her ex-husband, Mack, is repeatedly ordered first to stay and then to go, as Dee fights with "the animal" inside her that blocks her ability to love. The second, Toilane, is the uneducated superintendent of her apartment building, who becomes obsessed with her. Dee has an affair with him, then rejects him, although she is pregnant with his child. He wants her to give the baby to him when it is born, but she would rather give it to a stranger. In the end, the baby is kidnapped by Toilane and his mother, Pegs. Dee's sister, Mercy, suffers from the same kind of selfishness as Dee, but lacks her talent for bewitching men. Audiences have found *I Am Yours* stunning, overwhelming. Thompson feels that it has "a stronger narrative" than her other plays, but adds, "I wrote the plot in a day."

Given this speed of craft, and her audience's steady appetite for what she has to say, why have we seen only three Judith Thompson plays in eight years? The playwright explains: "The whole of *I Am Yours* is composed of collected images.... It takes me years to collect images. I'm like Pippi Longstocking. I see something in the subway. I hear about a friend's grand-mother. A lot of people—this terrifies me—assume that my plays are confessional, autobiographical somehow. I would never be so dreary as to bore the public with my own life or problems."

While she is busy collecting, ready to "steal my stories from anywhere," the subject of Thompson's next play is slowly forming somewhere deep within her unconscious. The images she acquires are "all covering, decoration—packaging—for the substance." "The substance is an ineffable kind of thing that I'm pursuing, that I know is inside me." But this secret sense of the play is never explicit for Thompson while she is writing; in fact, she admits that it does not really become clear for her until it is formulated "by journalists or friends or actors…. When I read the theatre press release, I know it's about obsession."

One of the strongest images in *I Am Yours* is the noise behind the wall of Mack's bookstore. The bookstore workers are bothered by a mysterious hum from one side of the room. When all the usual possibilities have been examined, and the hum persists, the wall is torn down to reveal an enormous beehive—a hidden, intensely active insect society operating just below the surface of the characters' lives, never quite encroaching, but always there. This rich metaphor found its way into *I Am Yours* because a friend of Thompson's had heard of such a beehive, discovered behind a judge's chamber wall. Thompson used the image "without really understanding what it meant to the play." She is, she says with pride and gratitude, not nearly as smart as her unconscious: "I feel really lucky that all these things connect."

Thompson hazards that, perhaps, her mind works in these mysterious ways because of her epilepsy. Although she has "experienced only one seizure in the past 15 years, Thompson wonders if this may be the explanation for the strong link she feels to her unconscious. "You have to be in contact with the dark," she says; she calls her condition "a mixed blessing." She describes herself and the way she thinks with the metaphor of a "screen door swinging between the unconscious and conscious mind," and candidly agrees that she is not, perhaps, entirely stable: a screen door is not a particularly solid partition.

Clare Coulter, who gave memorable performances in both of Thompson's last two plays, agrees with the playwright's assessment of her own creative powers. For Coulter, the plays are "surreal because they deal with the subconscious before the conscious has had a chance to order it safely." The power of Thompson's writing, Coulter adds, and her experience of playing Pony in *White Biting Dog*, "made me feel I should examine the way I approach my life." Thompson agrees that this is the effect she wants her art to have: "When it works best, it's cathartic. People feel completely released; they're shaking. That's the best reaction, the one I like best. When people say, 'Oh, I was quite impressed,' I want to punch them in the face."

Thompson's plays do have the kinds of moments she describes, when the audience is swept away by the beauty or the emotion of the scene. For me, the most powerful moment in all of Thompson's plays comes near the end of *White Biting Dog*. Pony, who is dead—she has just hanged herself—appears at the movie house in Kirkland Lake where her father works as a projectionist so that she can warn him of the tragic news he is about to receive. She wants to explain her action to him, "in person." Staring into the beam of light from the projector, as the movie continues to run, Pony reassures her father about death:

> It's quite nice, if you just give in to it. You know the feeling when you're falling asleep and ya jump awake 'cause you dreamt you slipped on a stair? Well, it's like if you stayed in the slip—if you dove right down into it and held your breath until you came out the other end. I'm in the holding your breath part right now, so I'm not sure what's on the other end, but I feel like I'm so big I'd barely fit into Kirk Community Centre....

Bill Glassco, who directed *White Biting Dog*, locates the appeal of Thompson's writing in the way it brings back the sensations of lost childhood. Glassco praises her imagination: "It connects me to a way I experienced the world in my own imagination when I was a child. The names—Lomia, Cape Race, Glidden, Toilane—they are like the names of people I invented as a child, who had complete biographies and were absolutely real to me. They say dangerous and shocking and silly things that for me express the unleashed anarchy of a child's mind. In the theatre this language is at once disturbing (because it connects with raw, primitive, forbidden emotions) and liberating (hence positive). This is how I believe her plays weave their spell."

Thompson develops her poetic revelations and embodies them in vividly eccentric characters, always with a view to how the script must be realized on stage. She exercises a creator's vision so complete that it can strike an actor as authoritarian. The published version of *White Biting Dog*, for instance, carries this warning:

> Because of the extreme and deliberate musicality of this play, any attempts to go against the textual rhythms, such as the breaking up of an unbroken sentence, or the taking of a pause where none is written in are DISASTROUS. The effect is like being in a small plane and suddenly turning off the ignition....

Thompson vigorously defends this demanding attitude as her prerogative: "In a first production the mandate must be to fulfill the playwright's vision. I think that's really important because it'll probably never be fulfilled again. When I write a play I know the characters as well as I know my own mother or father. If I wrote lines that my father would say, and you said, 'Well, I see him with a pipe,' I'd have to say, 'No, actually he doesn't smoke a pipe; he chain-smokes cigarettes.' I'd just have to... It's all inside you... as if it's a reincarnation."

Thompson "got into a lot of trouble over this last production" because of the strictness of her specifications. "Actors feel a bit straitjacketed sometimes," she acknowledges. "They're used to dead playwrights. With them; they have to make a lot of it up; they have to do a lot of guesswork. You know, Richard III is actually gay, or something like that.... Who knows what Shakespeare thought?" For her perfectionism, Thompson has been barred from dressing rooms after opening night—many actors do not appreciate getting notes from the playwright, night after night, about what they should do to finally get it *right*.

Bill Glassco, directing *White Biting Dog,* had to deal with Thompson's demand that a director walk a fine line with her plays and found himself caught between the writer and the performers: "The actors must feel a part of the creative process, as opposed to feeling they are simply the playwright's tools. As I recall, I encouraged Judith to explain and expound on the meaning of any given moment, but discouraged her from telling the actors or showing them how to realize it. Her understanding is invaluable to the actor, her excluding them from the creative process, destructive.... It is never easy. It is often exhausting, but because her plays are what they are, the challenge for a director is extraordinary, and I wouldn't have missed it." Not all theatre people, however, are troubled by the determined Thompson approach: Clare Coulter has worked on new plays and classics alike, and she muses, "Sometimes it would be nice to phone up Chekhov and ask about Nina."

Thompson will probably cut out the middleman altogether, with her next stage play, by directing it herself. Thompson did direct the New York production of *The Crackwalker* and was pleased with the results: "I understand my work better than anybody else. I also understand stagecraft pretty well, except I have to learn to do this fakey stuff, and say, 'Oh you were so brilliant there.'"

What that next play will be about, however, and when it will be written remain a mystery to Thompson. For now, she's collecting images for a feature film she's writing, and preparing for the birth of her second child, due in April. Writing while pregnant is difficult for Thompson; pregnancy, for her, fulfills certain needs that have otherwise motivated her writing. "It's like—if you have a full meal, why would you have anything else?"

But Thompson continues to write, and other possible connections between biology and writing occur to her. She never knows when an idea for a new script will attack the unconscious, invading her life: "I think it begins the same way a disease begins. One day a virus just toddles on into your body and starts to reproduce itself in the nucleus of your cells."

(1988)

Revisions of Probability:
An Interview with Judith Thompson
by Sandra Tomc

This interview took place on Tuesday, 24 January 1989 in Judith Thompson's home. The general question I was interested in pursuing was, what is it to be a woman writing for the theatre? We rapidly narrowed it down.

Sandra Tomc: You have two small children. When do you find time to write?

Judith Thompson: I hire a sitter every day from one to five. It is sort of difficult because writing for the theatre is not lucrative at all. In order to support my writing for the theatre I have to write for film. I have to do all this creepy television stuff.

ST: Why is it creepy?

JT: It's not a creative process at all—you're just a lackey and a dialogist and if you have any original thoughts those are the things they have trouble with. And you have these awful story conferences when they tell you what a character is really like and what they should be thinking and saying and all about structure. "I don't think that Jane would say it like this, Judith," they tell me and I feel like saying, "She only exists as far as I say, don't you understand?" It's like she's some kind of Frankenstein.

ST: Do you find that your two roles, playwright and mother, conflict at all?

JT: No, they feed into each other in a psychological way. I sometimes think that's why there aren't more women writers, because it's conventionally seen as a masculine thing to write. Especially a play.

ST: Why do you say, especially a play?

JT: Well, because a novel is more of a private thing and when you read it it's a private experience. But there's something about a play that's being "showy," which is thought of as a masculine thing—penetrating the audience. But then a mother is a very powerful thing too, you become a very powerful figure for your children.

ST: Do you think, then, there is such a thing as a feminine or feminist theatre?

JT: What they say, as I understand it—what some feminists say, for example, Cynthia Grant, although I may not be representing what she says properly, is that feminist theatre is ensemble theatre rather than "patriarchal" theatre. I don't agree with that at all. It's just powerful. That doesn't mean it's patriarchal. They think it's somehow fascistic to set up the word as king and then have the actors serve the word. I don't see it that way at all.

ST: What about actor/audience—or writer/audience—relationships? The way you described theatre at first was as a very powerful, very public medium. Do you think a feminist theatre would try to break down that power relationship?

JT: Yes, probably. You mean power in the sense that the play is penetrating the audience while they sit back passively?

ST: Yes.

JT: I like that, though. Just the way when you go to sleep you dream. They're your dreams, but it seems as if they're just happening to you. And that's what the ideal theatrical experience is for me. Feminists may say—the hardliners I mean, since I call myself a feminist—but they may say that that's too feminine. But men dream, we all dream, we all have an unconscious life. And I hope I have stumbled upon a kind of collective unconscious so that it's like a dream happening.

ST: But you like the idea that your plays have a certain "penetrative" effect.

JT: Yes! Well, in the sense that my plays happen to me, just like they happen to the audience. I remember one incident when a group of actors became infuriated—they were trying to analyze one of my plays intellectually. I kept insisting that although I could supply them with fifteen different interpretations now—because I'd finished writing the play—when I wrote it I didn't know what I was doing. And neither should you, I told them. I think they should just let it happen to them as it happened to me. I only become the "captain" in the rewrites. That's when I use all my experience in the theatre.

ST: Do you rewrite a lot?

JT: Lots. For about two years.

ST: So you first get together a skeleton which has all this unconscious power behind it?

JT: Not a skeleton, quite. Because a skeleton would be like a good outline.

ST: More like a series of vignettes?

JT: Sort of. I'll have three monologues, say, which really have caught fire or a collection of a whole bunch of images, or something that has been with me for a long time. Maybe I had a very manipulative friend when I was little and I've been thinking about that and I finally want to say something about what that manipulation is.

ST: Do you think of your work as feminist?

JT: No. I suppose you could interpret it that way. But I never think, oh I mustn't portray this woman as a weak woman, although some feminists believe that you should only have strong women. I'm not saying that what these feminists are promoting isn't good. It is good.

ST: Do you think your plays deal with women's issues?

JT: Not consciously. But they must because I'm a woman. It would be the same with any minority. It would have to be there in the writing somewhere.

ST: I'm just thinking of your three major works, *The Crackwalker*, *White Biting Dog* and *I Am Yours*. All of those plays deal centrally with sexuality and with the family. Do you think of these as women's issues?

JT: I don't think of them that way when I write. They're just what comes up on the page. Can you be more specific?

ST: Let's try a slightly different approach. Someone said to me once that they would hate to be inside your head. And there is, for instance, an horrific quality that surrounds your representations of sexuality.

JT: *(laughing)* Oh come on. It's not that bad.

ST: In *I Am Yours*, for example, you represent pregnancy in very nightmarish terms.

JT: Yes, and honestly, I have to say that I myself had a fantastic pregnancy. I wanted children. From the moment we decided to have children I wanted them desperately. Honestly. There was never a moment of ambiguity. I totally embraced it.

ST: So why do these nightmarish images emerge in your plays?

JT: I wanted to do a study of an amoral woman, Dee—I guess you could describe her as sociopathic—whose mother hated her and was jealous of her so she had no feeling for motherhood herself. She's terrified of anything taking over her, and this is represented by the animal behind the wall. So when that's translated into the body, she fears pregnancy because it is an idea that has always frightened her. She's the same with emotion. She's never allowed any real emotion to come to the surface and when it does come out, it takes this bizarre form: the way she is with her husband, go, stay, go, stay. I think I got the animal behind the wall image from children's nightmares about there being something in the closet. I always wonder though, when people say things like that—oh it must be horrible to be inside your head—who are they trying to kid that they don't have those things in their minds? Everybody has nightmares and everybody has terrible moments.

ST: What about your preoccupation with the family? Going back for a moment to what you said about Dee as a character who can't feel or deal with emotions: this is a fairly large issue in your plays—*White Biting Dog*, for instance.

JT: Yes … yes it is. Funny.

ST: This isn't something you set out to do?

JT: I don't know why it's there, I guess because I know a couple of people like that. There are lots of people like that. They're like the androids, the world is peppered with them. And usually it's people who are enchanting. As a psychiatrist I know said to me, anybody who charms me within twenty minutes is a psychopath. I thought that was very interesting. Of course, some people are just naturally charming, but not in that hypnotic way. When it's in that hypnotic way I think it's because the person stands back from people. It's the kind of person who notices too much about people right away—everything I'm wearing, what it says about me. I'm always very suspicious of people like that. If you're really interacting with someone you shouldn't be noticing these details. It's like when you're in love with someone, you don't notice strange things, but as soon as you're not in love with them everything is visible—except when you're a teenager. It's the same thing. You're standing back. You're not involved with them anymore. So these are people I find horrifying because they can distance themselves from a person and you think they're laughing with you but actually they're watching you. These are the kind of people who, if things go badly for them or they become enraged for some reason, become the Ted Bundys of the world.

ST: Is it significant that in *White Biting Dog* you place these characters in a family situation?

JT: I don't know. I suppose the family is obviously a microcosm of how you relate to the whole world. People who have been able to manipulate their parents manipulate the world and people for whom their parents were the ultimate authority tend to bow to other kinds of authority. The family is where I can really get in and study and investigate who people are.

ST: This is in reference to a conversation we had a while ago. Do you find male or female characters easier to develop?

JT: I find female characters easier. What I do have trouble with are characters who are not extraordinary in any way. I think I failed with Cape and with Dee, ultimately. I think I grasped character in the Aristotelian sense of what they do, and that is of course who they are. But characterization—for some reason I didn't go the whole route. I don't know why. It's easy enough. It's like Second City kind of stuff. You find the voice and then people love it. And then that's the way to lead them into who the character is. It's just the dressing, it's just getting dressed, basically. But often on my central characters … I think I have trouble with ordinary people who lead ordinary lives. Chekhov did wonderful things with ordinary people, although nobody is really ordinary of course. I just shave off the whole ordinary head and get underneath. Or *Thirty Something*. You can do wonderful things with ordinary people, and sometimes that show does. But I have trouble making them interesting. I've tried just to do middle class, ordinary people, but unless I can find some kind of speech rhythm, or something very different from me … If I try to do someone just like me or my family or you—it would just be very boring. I seem to have to have a trick. I really get annoyed with myself, but I have to. It's what the audience really responds to, too. I shouldn't call it a trick because it's not a thing I do knowingly, but all my characters, whether they're upper or lower class, have to have a quirk of some kind.

ST: Do you think that it's precisely because they are upwardly mobile middle class characters that you had problems with Cape and Dee?

JT: Yes. Whereas Lomia was more an aristocrat so I didn't have a problem with her because she had a flamboyant way of speaking. I don't exactly mean aristocrat, but she was used to privilege, she didn't care what people thought of her. Whereas middle class people care a lot. I kept working around speech patterns for Cape, coming up with different ones all the time and nothing really worked.

ST: What about issues of class? Do you consciously incorporate these?

JT: Yes, it's pretty important to me. In the best Shakespeare, for instance, I think, you always see both classes and it's a wonderful contrast to watch—almost just from a visceral point of view. It's like seeing black and red together. It's just good. But also class is so much a part of our society and culture—or every society and culture—I don't see how you could have a play without it. And if it's not class, it's status within a class. A guy named Keith Johnstone—he wrote a wonderful book called *Impro*—said that all plays are about power and changes in power. *Waiting for Godot*, Marx Brothers, what have you, all involve losing and gaining power. And I think all writers carry their childhood with them. I mean everybody does. That's where everything makes the deepest impression and that's when status and power are felt very keenly. That's when you're feeling where you are on the totem pole. I always tried to be in the middle because that's the best place to be, but occasionally I've also been on the top and the bottom and I remember being just as cruel as anybody when I was on the top. Anyway, I believe that all that exists in grown-ups. This is what I'm always looking at.

ST: How do you think that operates in the dynamic between, let's say, Cape and Pony?

JT: He's not intimidated by her in any way. He's probably not intimidated by any woman because he doesn't have the desire that most men have, which goes back to what I was saying about people who distance themselves. Pony obviously isn't as privileged as he is and he feels he can stand back and manipulate her because she's kind of quirky and funny. And of course when she falls in love with him, he's got it all over her. In a way that's representative of the whole of the upper class.

ST: So the class dynamic basically translates into the romance dynamic.

JT: It translates socially in the sense of everyone wanting to be like the rich and famous and falling in love with that. And the rich and famous are manipulating them. And the media manipulate the people who sit in front of their TVs day and night into wanting to be like that and so buying into the nonsense.

ST: How do male critics and theatre-goers respond to your plays? Do you think there's a difference in the way that men and women have responded?

JT: Men especially hated Dee because they obviously found her very threatening. And they hated Max, her husband. They called him a wimp. He wasn't a wimp. He was the only character capable of disinterested love. To see a woman pushing a man around like that really horrified them. They were just enraged. Now, there were a couple of men—writers—who empathized with her.

ST: Are you talking about critics here?

JT: No, audience. The critics for *I Am Yours* were positive, but I think that's just because by now I have some kind of reputation. People always assume, "Oh you must have got raves for *Crackwalker*," and I just got nothing but panned. There was maybe one good review. *Crackwalker* was completely panned here by all three papers. And then finally it went to Montreal and there was one critic there who loved it. And then it came back here and Gina Mallet was told by her entertainment editor—I keep saying this and nobody prints it and I want them to because he told me this—she was told by him that she had to make peace with Canadian theatre and forced her to write a good review. She wrote a glowing review of the play, which I guess was a complete lie. So really—her credibility … I always thought she was vicious but that she meant what she said. You asked me about male critics. Well, Gina Mallet was the cruelest critic of them all.

ST: This is for *Crackwalker*.

JT: And for *White Biting Dog*—she was even more cruel.

ST: What sort of things did she say?

JT: I didn't read that one because these things stay in my mind for too long. But it was very snide, and very much a who-did-I-think-I-was kind of feeling, like "Ooh, watch out for the bite of White Biting Dog." A lot of people think that my work is out to shock people. But I really am honestly shocked when people are shocked. It would be as if I said to you, "I heard an awful story about a lady down the street who has cancer," you know, just a sad story, and you said to me, "Oh Judith! Why did you want to shock me like that?!" You wouldn't say that, would you. You'd feel for this lady.

ST: Maybe it's the unusual way in which you express these stories that shocks people. Your language is unusual.

JT: Yeah, I guess … Is it unusual, the language?

ST: It's unexpected.

JT: You mean like when Toy says, "I want to be your knight with no armour?" Strange language like that? Idiosyncratic?

ST: That's not quite what I mean. I'm just trying to think of an example … from *White Biting Dog*, say ...

JT: That's the toughest play.

ST: How do you mean, the toughest?

JT: It's the least accessible. It's got more in it, it's more worth studying carefully than the others. There's about five layers. And I'd say *I Am Yours* is about three. *Crackwalker* is really what it is—not that it's not as good, but it's what it is. I worked hardest on *White Biting Dog*.

ST: Has *White Biting Dog* had the most ambivalent response from people?

JT: Probably. But a lot of people like it the best.

ST: It's the most extreme, I think.

JT: It is the most extreme but—and this is how I used to always defend it—anything in it, except Pony coming back from the dead, of course, could happen. People don't listen, though, you know. A couple of people have said to me "What happens to Pony?" And yet Pony says several times, "The reason I killed myself …" Plus she has a rope around her neck. It's very clear. But people don't listen. Once they think the play is weird, that's it. But the story's just right there. There's nothing strange, really. Here's a man who was just going to commit suicide, he hallucinated a dog—as many crazy people do—telling him he had a mission. They're all over the place, people with missions. And yet for some reason, people think, "This is odd, so I'm not to take anything seriously." But then that's my responsibility. I have to finally realize that anything that's on stage is amplified about a hundred times, that anything would be ordinary in conversation is extraordinary on stage.

ST: Let's talk about *Crackwalker* for a minute. What was behind your characterization of Theresa?

JT: Most people see Theresa as a victim … because she's a prostitute, she sucks off queers at the Lido for five dollars, lives on couches or with any man that takes her in. But I always saw her as kind of a real happy character. A survivor, though in a sense I hate that word. There's one reference to her being Indian and I was talking to a Native Canadian once and I said, "She digests the horror of her baby being killed and then she moves on. It's not that she feels it any less or that she felt it any less at the time." And he said, "Well that's a very Indian thing." I didn't know that when I wrote the play. But then a lot of my work is luck. A lot of it's luck—like a frightening amount of it is luck.

ST: What's your own family background?

JT: My parents are both professors. My father was head of the Department of Psychology at Queen's, my mother taught English there for a while but mainly was a mother—and a writer, and she worked as a director when she was younger, and an actress. So I've had access to a sort of middle class life, but access to upper as well because my mother's father was the Prime Minister of Australia for a while and the Ambassador to Canada and she went to private schools and all that stuff. The people she was friends with in college became very rich people and married very rich people, so we'd stay in their houses. And then I also at the same time went to a tough Catholic elementary school in Kingston. You know, people who would knock over *Globe and Mail* boxes when they were eleven, twelve years old and stayed out all night and they'd be exhausted in class. There were a couple of other daughters of professionals in the class, but mainly it was Kingston underprivileged.

ST: Did that experience provide you with the background to write about someone like Theresa?

JT: Theresa actually came from a job I had as an adult protective services worker's assistant one summer when I was at NTS and there was a girl who was borderline mentally handicapped and she had this wonderful way of speaking and a wonderful purity about her. I based Theresa on her. Theresa doesn't speak like Kingston uneducated. That's Alan more, or Sandy.

ST: You mentioned that you didn't think of Theresa as a victim. Do you think that her ability to digest tragedy, as you called it, is part of her status as a victim? Doesn't she do that because she has to, because she can't afford to be neurotic or even sad about it?

JT: Well, it depends on how you work within the system. She could have been hysterical about it and then she would have been in a nice comfortable hospital. But that's not who she is—she's not that unhappy. She's not unhappy. That's the thing about her that's interesting. In a sense, Joe is the same way. Sandy's not. She's trying very hard to be middle class and not quite making it. She's very "a place for everything and everything in its place." "No, you're not retarded, you're just slow." Things like that. Everything is set out for her, everything in its place. She has to be that way or she falls into the abyss the crackwalker. "The crackwalker don't hurt nobody," that's what she says. That's how she's reassured herself. "I learned how to make a new drink"—that's a big thing for her. We haven't really been very feminist.

(1989)

A Conversation with Judith Thompson
by Cynthia Zimmerman

Cynthia Zimmerman: In an earlier interview you said that writers carry their childhood with them. Would you expand on that?

Judith Thompson: Well, I shouldn't generalize about all writers, but I think the reason I did is because so often when I've read writers that have touched me I know that I've related to something from the child in them, or in their protagonist, which has touched the child in me. I think it's because I see growing up in this culture as a process of throwing great coats of civilization over true responses. So when I say "carry our childhood with us" I mean still express true emotional responses.

CZ: I thought perhaps you were referring to the Freudian idea that the past is always present. I was connecting it to your Roman Catholic upbringing and the religiosity in your work.

JT: It'll be very interesting to see what happens to my work now because I haven't been to church in about sixteen years. I'm getting farther and farther away from it. I don't really remember what you do when you go into a church now. For *Lion in the Streets* I got the stage manager to go and find out how it went. Though the priest doesn't say it in Latin anymore, I had wanted whatever the priest says when the person goes into the box to be in Latin.

CZ: Do you think your plays—most noticeably in *Lion in the Streets*—express a religious sensibility?

JT: Oh yes, it's very much a part of my life. I just assume it's a part of everybody's. For me there is a constant struggle inside—a sort of St. George and the Dragon—going on all the time. Was this an evil thought? Was this a good thought? War, for example. I just saw an amazing documentary on the massacre at My Lai in Vietnam. They actually interviewed men in the company, and they interviewed survivors. It was so graphic! People say, "This happens all the time, Judith," and of course it does, but it was so detailed, and the details were so compelling. I've been literally tortured. For the last two weeks that is all I've been thinking about. Now we have the war in Iraq. This is drama! This is a function for drama in a sense because the war in Iraq is being shown to us like some kind of Nintendo game. We haven't seen the seven-year-old boy wandering without arms ... I mean the *real* details that bring it home. Now it's an abstraction like all wars were when I was a child, or like other people's divorces. But that massacre lives with me and I force myself in a kind of Jesuit way to go through it, to experience what the victims experienced. Perhaps it's masochistic but I feel it's my duty as a human being, and as an artist. It feels devastating, needless to say. Of course I can't suffer one-millionth of what the victims suffered, but I try. I feel it's our duty as dramatists to bring the world closer, just as that documentary brought that event up front and centre for me.

CZ: This is reminding me of a play called *Plugged into History*, written by John McGrath years ago. The notion of *Plugged into History* was a woman who *felt* the newspaper reports.

JT: I do too. It's the R.D. Laing idea that maybe the people who are walking around muttering and who seem crazy to us are the people who feel the world the most intensely. When I am working I have to be able to separate myself: I have to be able to "go in" and "out" constantly. I need to "go out" and see whether it's way too long, or its way over the top, or whatever, but I have to "go in" for it to "be there," for it to be inspired.

CZ: When your characters struggle the message seems to be that people do do terrible things, but it's not their fault. There's another reading behind the moral structure which indicates that their behaviour is not just an action, it's a reaction.

JT: Oh, of course. This is the big struggle about Marc Lepine. Is it Marc Lepine, or is he just this little waste product? This social body? Of course that doesn't excuse him.

CZ: Do you think there's a "through line" to the concerns expressed in your work?

JT: There's definitely not a conscious one. The only way that I can work well is to wait for it to happen and then shape it afterwards. I never shape it intellectually, its always done instinctively, like shaping music. And it's really not until long afterwards that I talk about it with people. I learn from those talks because others find things that are there, because I think that I have responded to a kind of collective pool—a kind of collective unconscious.

CZ: Are you deliberately using a Jungian term?

JT: Well, he gave it a name, but it is something I have felt anyway. You become aware of an amazing sort of synchronicity going on when you talk to other artists, or cross time. Its the opposite of the Marxist view that everything is contextual. The idea is that people in, say, Egypt, thousands of years ago, reacted in the same way that people now do to certain things. I believe that. Otherwise, I'd just give up. I really believe that if the thing is clear enough there is an emotional sameness in the response to it. Everyone likes babies, for example, and you can start with things as primitive and obvious as that. But to return to your question about religion … certainly in the Catholic religion the struggle between Satan and God is a constant thing. Also the Catholic religion has this immense kind of poetry—Bernadette, and the Lady appearing to Bernadette, and all the pomp and ceremony. Like every little girl I just loved all that. It's interesting, though, that in the Catholic christening service the priest says to the baby, "Do you reject Satan and all his pomp and ceremony?" Funny. But all those images in the church, all those windows make this moral struggling seem very real.

CZ: To return to my question of the presence of your past in your work, was there a connection to the death of your father in *White Biting Dog*?

JT: My father's death was in *The Crackwalker*. In a little section where Alan talks about his father dying of lung cancer there were details that were true and, of course, the despair about it. But the rest is unrelated to my own life. In *White Biting Dog* it would be Pony's relationship to her father that was probably the closest. Her father the projectionist—my father was a psychologist. But mainly it's the closeness, her bond. The way she says, "I wish my dad was here and would spit on his hanky"—that kind of memory. Maybe unconsciously I wished I could have saved him somehow, but I don't think that was there so much. I was drawing on the death of an acquaintance, a friend who jumped off a bridge. I needed something to pull it together. I still find it a little clumsy; I sort of wince when that part comes in the text and I want it to be over. I do. I tend to be too linear. I'm finding that in writing films: I have to stop explaining. Of course, most of my audience would disagree. They always think, "What's going on?" And I love the words anyway … that's what I hate about film. They just keep saying, "Cut back, cut back, cut back." Then I see those wonderful old Hitchcock films and there are plenty of words, and I say, "But, but…" to them.

CZ: What is your process for getting started? Do you keep a sort of mental filing cabinet?

JT: It is mental but there are actual monologues and bits and pieces in a filing cabinet. I don't do that much anymore. But it might be something that I didn't use in another play that I always wanted to, or something observed, or something heard, something remembered, and sometimes a whole play will be structured around, say, four pieces that I really wanted to use. Then I try to figure out a sort of algebraic equation. Rather like the old fable about nail soup. You know, the one where the fellow comes to town and says, "Well, you have no money? I'll make you an amazing soup with just a nail! Bring me a nail,… now bring me a carrot,… now bring me a potato …" and so on. Then you remove the nail. That's where the magic comes in. Finally you could take out the four pieces, and you could take out the algebraic equation. The magic in between is what the play is.

If you don't start with a pre-conceived structure, the structure emerges more intuitively, like a piece of music. That's much better. Content *is* structure. In contrast, with film you're supposed to create a "this happens, then this happens." It's a well-made play kind of thing. So it's generally "so what?" When the structure cannot equal the content, then it can only be what the story is, and you can get that from any television movie any night of the week.

CZ: My sense is that the drive in your plays is supplied by your characters.

JT: They structure it. I hate to impose structure; I find that so false. So I think structure is a wonderful thing, I love how this scene comes after this other kind of scene and dips up, and so on. I love form and shape and I love to move bodies on stage. I think that equals content, as Aristotle would say, but not in his way.

CZ: Do you deliberately experiment with form or structure?

JT: Sometimes. I know that in *The Crackwalker* I just felt my way. I had no idea what I was doing. Except I was a bit influenced, I think, by Mamet's *Sexual Perversity in Chicago*. I had just done a little thing of that in the summer with some friends. It was the episodic nature of it, and I also think his freedom with four-letter words freed me. In *White Biting Dog* I wanted to do something well-made. I worked hard on that. And then in *I Am Yours* I crossed between the two in an odd way. It still had that narrative pull. Although people will say, "What's the story here?" to me it is sound, almost too sound. And then with *Lion in the Streets* I was sitting here, having to write a radio play that was commissioned—actually, I'm in a similar predicament right now—and I couldn't think of a thing to do. I thought I just can't bear some giant narrative, somebody taking this immense journey. So I thought, well, write a bunch of little plays, like two women in a restaurant and one says, "Guess what?" I had no idea what it was going to be. It was an improvisation, basically. And I always work best that way. When I'm inside the characters, I have no idea what's going to come next. And with the two women in the restaurant out came this beautiful Ophelia speech. So that's the way for me. I can't know what I'm going to do beforehand.

CZ: How do you know when it's finished?

JT: It's never finished. It's only finished when I'm sick of it. For the radio play I've got a deadline, but as far as a stage play, it's finished when I stop wincing.

CZ: When you're writing do you have a particular theatre in mind? Do you have this [Tarragon] theatre in mind?

JT: Physically? Pretty well, yes, now I do. I didn't at first at all. I had nothing but a blackness, voices in the black. Earlier I did seem to close off the visual part of myself, which is funny because I like exploring visual imagery and I have a facility with it. Now I think I'm exploring it more and more. Even though *Lion in the Streets* was originally a radio play, so it was kind of limited, when I was directing it for the stage I had to visualize more and more.

CZ: Why did you choose to start directing your own work?

JT: With all due respect to the people who have directed my plays in the past, I really have always directed my premieres. I've co-directed them, and I've done so much of the talking that I've always felt as if I were virtually directing it. So I thought, "This is stupid." And actor-friends said the same thing: "Direct it yourself. You know exactly what to do. You know how to move people on stage." I was a bit overbearing and overcontrolling at first. That's something I really had to learn through workshop. At the University of New Brunswick I directed *The Crucible* where it was okay to be overbearing with first and second-year students. But through the workshop of *Lion in the Streets*, and then in rehearsals, I had to learn to give actors their freedom, I had to try to be constructive without being critical.

CZ: I wondered how you walked that line.

JT: It's very difficult since I know exactly what I want. Mind you, I do like to be surprised. If someone like Stephen Ouimette comes along he can do things I had no notion of; he can find a million things I didn't even know were there! I would rarely admit this, but when I watched him I saw him create a hundred nuances for my one. He is almost dangerous for a writer because you don't change anything. When he is performing you think, "That's great writing", and then someone else does it—even someone that's very good—and then you realize it's not great without him.

    Usually when reviews say, "The performances were great, but the writer wasn't," I would say, "That's impossible. You can't get a great performance from bad writing." Well, I do still think it's impossible, but actors like Stephen definitely elevate the material.

CZ: After you have directed your premiere production, is that when your involvement stops?

JT: Yes, I love to see what other people do to it.

CZ: What did other people do with the 1990 remount of *White Biting Dog*, at the Grand Theatre?

JT: I really liked it. It wasn't that different from the one done here. Maja Ardal directed it and she must have had a great sensitivity to the writing, to the demands of it, because nobody went against the grain.

CZ: What about the recent French production of *I Am Yours* in Montreal?

JT: That was very different. They approached it as a piece of rock and roll. It was great, but I don't know if I would have thought so if it had been in English. It was bizarre. For instance, they had this poster of a Gerber baby from the fifties with this odd smile. It said, "I Am Yours," and had a bow wrapped around its neck. Still, the production worked. What's really of substance in the text stands up. It will always stand up no matter how you paint the building or how you dress things up.

CZ: I wanted to ask you about the different versions of the baby-murder scene in *The Crackwalker*. The Playwrights Canada version came out in 1981 and may go out of print. Now there is the 1989 Coach House Press collected plays, *The Other Side of the Dark*. Looking at the two scripts it is clear there has been extensive rewriting. It was the Coach House Press version, wasn't it, that was recently mounted at the Tarragon? Was the one at the Tarragon a return to the 1980 version, a version that was altered for the 1981 publication?

JT: Yes it was, specifically the build-up to the murder. The murder was always offstage, until the Tarragon production. But the original build-up to it stressed the societal forces acting upon Alan—the goddam social workers, the doctors, the medicines, the job, the you won't make love to me anymore "cause he said so"—all these forces were crucial. And this is how it really happened when there was a murder of a baby while I was working in Kingston for the Ministry of Social Services. The people weren't those characters at all. But there was a couple with a baby and the wife phoned and told me the baby had died. She told me how it happened. When she was directing it in London Maja Ardal shoved this old script in front of me and said, "What about this version?" I read it and realized that the Playwrights Canada version had been my reaction to the press's pigeonholing me, saying that I was a tape-recorder-kind-of-writer. And I thought, no, I'm lyrical, I'm a poet. I think I tried to make that scene more poetic in reaction. And it was wrong because it made Alan a madman rather than presenting his actions as resulting from the forces acting on him. I think there may be a touch of madness in his character, but it is more all these forces.

CZ: As in *The Crackwalker*, in subsequent plays the individual's crisis is placed within its social context. In your most recent play, *Lion in the Streets*, the lion that is in the streets clearly connects to the lion within. But what exactly is that connection?

JT: Well, I mean the lion within running wild, set free. That's a theme in *I Am Yours* as well. The lion is something buried, a force that can be great or terrible. We've buried it for so long that when it comes out it comes out roaring, like a caged animal.

CZ: The lion has a place in this world, but it belongs somewhere else? not in the street?

JT: In a civilized place the street is paved.

CZ: Do you think that the cruelties present in each of the episodes in *Lion in the Streets* are connected to the ultimate tragedy?

JT: They are a series of soul murders or physical murders. Yes, they are all related. As I was saying about the moral struggle I have every day, I always feel that even talking about someone behind their back in a certain way can be a kind of murder. What you're doing is cutting off any empathic cord. You treat them as if they are an object, as if they have no humanity. Those acts are little murders. We are connected to that child murderer. And we are connected to the guys at My Lai.

CZ: Don't we have to separate carelessness and those little cruelties from violent psychotic behaviour? After all, while there may be many little murders, most people don't go over the edge and a lot of your characters do. What makes them different?

JT: Well, I think most people do go over the edge internally, or everybody has extremely shocking stories to tell, or have had moments that seem ordinary at first, but when you examine them they are profoundly shocking. You know what I mean? Things like betrayals. But the bringing together of the vignettes in *Lion in the Streets* was never conscious. I never thought, okay, now I'm going to connect. I didn't even know it was about Isobel until the last couple of months. I finally realized that, of course, the killer in the graveyard was her killer. It just came to me. It's like an *idiot savante* or something, or like me clearing a window. Like it's there and I'm finding it.

CZ: When Isobel says, "Take back your life, take back your life," what does that mean to you? What do you want me to hear?

JT: I guess so many of us allow ourselves to be victims; we let the blood be sucked out of us. It's as if there's a giant straw and I want to say, "suck it back!"

CZ: Don't let it happen. But a lot of things the victim could do nothing about. Like bone cancer, or that little girl. What could she do about it, just a little girl?

JT: I know. And how does she take back her life by forgiving him? I mean, it is mysterious. By forgiving him she becomes the stronger one.

I don't share it, but people who believe in reincarnation have an interesting attitude to death and dying. One passes on to something, rather than just being the victim of this growth, this cancer, or whatever. The belief that you're strong, that you're able to shed this and go on—I really think that in many areas it is possible to turn our sense of being victims around. Of course I do know how out of control things can go, and how fast it can happen. Like my own epilepsy, or watching my father's lung cancer. So I do try to keep everything smooth. But at times I feel I'm a helpless victim, and totally incompetent in the animate world. Maybe a part of me wants to draw this state out and not take responsibility. Also, I know that the way my work works is from a kind of chaos, a helpless chaos. And that I have to feel passive, like a conduit. I don't want to do too much directing because of that. As soon as I start to feel queenly, I know something will go away.

CZ: You want to retain a kind of vulnerability?

JT: That's right, it has to be. If not, I'm in trouble.

CZ: Do you feel bolder about what you can experiment with or take on?

JT: About the same, or maybe a little less. I'm now conscious that I can lose people, and that I don't need to lose them if I just change a few things. It's not really compromising at all. I'm not going to build a little gilded bridge to reach them, but I am trying to reach people. I don't want to alienate them.

CZ: Do you have a favourite play?

JT: I love them all; they are like my children. They all have things about them that I might love more or love less, but no, actually, I love everything about them. I love watching them go on to their own next life. It's just great seeing them, and interesting and bizarre. Sometimes I think, who wrote that? Where did that come from? It's like seeing children grow, as if there's another whole independent human being. It's wonderful.

CZ: What would you like the audience to take home?

JT: First, a kind of intensity about being alive, about living in the world at this moment—good art does that for me. Then I would like them to experience the painful thing of looking in the mirror, even if the characters aren't like them in superficial ways. So if, for example, when people see Christine beating up Scarlett in *Lion in the Streets*, if rather than saying "she's crazy," they say, "When have I felt that kind of explosive hostility? And why? And what's going on?" It's a kind of forced confrontation with the self. My real hope is to hold a mirror up to all of us, because I think that awakening, slipping out of our comas, is what it's all about. Otherwise, we do not live—it's the unexamined life. The coma lifting, then, becomes political. Art is political, should be political, but only in this really essential way.

CZ: Not a particular platform?

JT: It's not at all about a particular platform. You have to change your whole sense of who you are in the world. See that you are an active and effective person in the world. See that you can actually make a difference. Isobel says, "Take back your life." "I will no longer be a victim. I won't be sent to war. I will take back my life." That's the way I make a political statement. I don't have to say something specific or current.

CZ: How would you define a good critic?

JT: When I'm most excited by critics is when they find "islands" in the play, things that come up like hidden Atlantises and then they connect them to other islands. And when they can see clearly and can share it, like Northrop Frye helping people to appreciate Blake. It seems to me very important to read writers like Blake, because they help us see clearly, they help give life meaning. They help us see through the everydayness into what is profound, enduring, lasting.

CZ: Finally, what are you working on now?

JT: A half-hour radio play commissioned to coincide with the Women Playwrights Conference—I am completely stuck, and it's due very soon. And I'm adapting *Hedda Gabler* for the Shaw Festival production which I am directing this summer. I've sort of been working on another play as well, in a kind of unconscious scattered way. But it's coming. I've just handed in a second draft of the film script for *I Am Yours*, but I'm squabbling with the story editor so I'm feeling rather negative about it. I have no objectivity on that right now.

CZ: Are you making a living as a writer?

JT: As a screenwriter, not as a playwright.

(1990)

One Twelfth

by Judith Thompson

It was about six a.m. on a May Sunday morning and I awoke with a question shaking my brain: "Where are the eleven other Judiths?" It was not just the question that frightened me, rather the profound feeling of being one-twelfth of a whole, of being totally without a centre. The only common sensation I can compare it to is waking up in a strange bed and not remembering where you are for a very long minute. But this was much scarier. My head ached for the rest of the day, and I wondered if this was insanity. I looked into yoga classes, thinking they might calm me down, and I even saw a therapist, who suggested that my roles as writer, wife, mother, friend, daughter, etc. etc. were dividing me, and that I needed to find the "Mick Yagger" (she was Scandinavian) in me to pull them all together. I told her I would think about that, but when I did, I realized that these eleven others were not my various functions as a female person in this society, but me. Essential pieces of me which I have cut away and planted in my work, to watch them grow and expand like those creepy instant caves that suddenly grow dozens of stalactites and stalagmites upon immersion in water. I saw myself as a giant earthworm with a cutting knife lopping off bits of itself to grow new worms in the ground. Like a Faustian trade, these new worms brought success and recognition, but what was happening to the original worm? What good is success when you're only a twelfth? And how many times can you divide one twelfth, and still grow good worms? I decided that in order to continue as a writer, I just had to have faith that the wriggling one twelfth would again become the big strong earthworm it once was, despite all the missing pieces. And I just had to stop thinking about worms.

In preparation for this essay, I tried to look at my characters from a feminist perspective. To be honest, I wasn't exactly sure what I was looking for, but what I saw is that none of my characters defines herself as a feminist, or as someone opposed to feminism. Most of them have been successfully brainwashed by the patriarchal society in which they live, and the others are in a fight to the death with themselves because of it. But there is one I have overlooked, I think, waiting patiently at the back of the crowd, her legs crossed at the ankle, watching me. She is waiting for me to see her. I will look at her now.

"How come you're so fuckin' ugly?" Red-faced and wild-haired on her bike, with old green sweat pants and a colourless ripped and stained pullover, she smiles reflexively, and then burns dark red when she realizes that she has been insulted.

She makes a disgusted face at the boys, but what she really wants to do is get off her bike and go down on her knees and say, "Please, please, I know I don't look great today, but honestly, my boyfriend thinks I'm beautiful, and other boys have even said it too! Honest!" A few months later, she is walking up University Avenue in a pretty dress, hair clean and brushed, makeup just right, when several American businessmen here on a day-trip spy her and shout something. Their faces look friendly and it is spring, so she gives them her most girlish smile, until she finally understands what they are saying. They are saying, "At last, a six and a half! Alright!" She gives them the finger and marches away, thinking "Six and a half, is that all? God what a self deluded fool, here all this time I've thought of myself as a seven and a half, sometimes even an eight." When she was a child she agreed with her father when he pointed out that women had achieved very little of consequence in the history of the world, and were therefore not equal. After all, even the best *chefs*, he said, pleased with himself, are male. Not only did she agree with this, but she spouted it to anybody who would listen. When the same father claimed that his wife, her mother, was clearly his intellectual superior, his daughter was truly puzzled, and lost. When she was a teen, she and her friends agreed—over many a french fries and gravy in the mall "lunchspot"—that they all wanted a boy who was more intelligent than they were, a boy who would "take charge." They had bitter contempt for the poor fool who would ask them what they might like to do on a Saturday night; instead, they wanted a boy who would take them by the hand like a four-year-old, and when the time came, throw them down on the bed, *certainly never* ask, "May I kiss you." That was repulsive and weak. They broke any kind male heart, dropping him at the first glimmer of goodness, with a sharp, "You're just too nice, that's all." The kind of boys they went for only liked one thing about girls, and they weren't nice.

Now she is all grown up, an unfeminist feminist; she and her husband do equal portions of the child care and housework, true, but, it is he who puts out the garbage, always, and picks up the maggot-covered mouse corpses that litter the house after they lay down poison. It is he who lays down the poison. It is he who cleans the toilet (once or twice a decade) and she who nags him to do it. She also nags him to mow the lawn, because she can't because she has no energy left after running five miles a day. Pretty well any socializing they do is arranged by her, and when they have guests it is she who directs the clean up and designs the meal. If they are attending a special event it is she who decides what the children will wear. It is she who writes the thank you notes, and buys his mother birthday presents. She does not, however, iron his shirts. He does all that paperwork and mailing involved in paying the bills—she doesn't even know who they pay their mortgage to, or really, what a mortgage is. There is a lot she doesn't know, considering the kind of books she reads. In fact, she knows nothing at all about any traditionally male things. She doesn't know how to fix a car, or check an engine, she doesn't even know how to fix her own bike. She doesn't really know how radios or TVs work, and instead of considering herself a seriously handicapped person, she excuses herself because she is a woman.

In her most erotic dreams, she is very passive.

Her daughter somehow has five or six Barbie dolls, and her son is obsessed with all things mechanical. She is not quite sure how this happened. She hates Barbie, she is a feminist. She doesn't even shave her legs, although her own growth is very sparse, and when she does see a woman with a luxuriant growth of hair on legs or under armpits, it makes her want to throw up. She doesn't believe in makeup, but she has a lot more confidence when she is wearing it. She loses her confidence easily. A cold remark can result in hours of late-night tears and self-hatred. She would not, however, tolerate this weakness in her husband. She would find it repulsive. In the early days of their courtship he sometimes sat with his legs together, tucked up underneath him. She would chide him, and demand that he sit with his legs apart, like other men.

She is uncomfortable with beautiful women, and at times has experienced monstrous jealousy towards them, hating them for their gifts, and wishing them ill fortune. She feels very happy, however, with fat or "ugly" women, because she is not threatened by them. Inwardly, she feels superior to the "ugly" women, and inferior to the beautiful. She hates herself for this.

Because she lacks confidence, she wants to be liked. In order to be liked, she is overly agreeable. Once, when she and her beautiful cousin were looking at a dress in a store window, she remarked that she loved the dress. Her cousin hated the dress. She, then, decided that she hated it too. Her cousin challenged her. "Well," she said, "it's just that I see your point of view." Her cousin lost all respect for her, but this didn't matter, really, as long as they agreed. She needed to agree with whomever she was with, and consequently sat on the fence on most issues. On abortion: she had one years ago, for convenience, and will never forgive herself. She knows that abortion is better than thirteen-year-olds having babies or killing themselves with Drano and coat hangers, but she is horrified by it as a birth-control method. She considers herself a murderer because of her own abortion. She just doesn't know what to think; she would not march with pro-choice, because abortion on demand is really so repellent to her, but she would never ally herself with the right-wingers and warmongers that seem to make up the right-to-lifers. She is deeply ashamed of her lack of commitment, but finally, she would rather sit on this barbed-wire fence than jump down on either side. This is because she knows that if she jumped down on the side of her heart, not only would she lose her friends, but she would have to work very hard for support for unwed mothers and unwanted children, she would have to write letters, make phone calls, give lunches and raise money for the rest of her life. She is not willing to do that. Her privacy and leisure are more important than her deeply held beliefs. She hates herself for this.

She cannot really be trusted with a secret, because telling an important secret gives her such focused attention and power. She always says, to the three or four people she tells, "You mustn't tell *anybody*" and she hopes that they won't, not because she is too concerned about the people involved, but because she doesn't want to get in trouble. She has even told one or two girlfriends very personal things about her relationship with her husband, but she would never forgive him if he breathed a word about her to anybody.

She is afraid of everything: jobs, supermarkets, malls, tough boys, cancer, and being alone. Most of all, being alone. She identified with the old woman she read about who had buried four husbands but now lived by herself: naked in her cold apartment, she would phone her grandchildren at work dozens of times a day, screaming that she was dying of loneliness and that they had to come right that second, she couldn't be alone, she couldn't stand it. "Hurry, please, you can't leave me alone! You can't! You can't! You can't leave me alone!"

She sees herself in that old woman, but feels that she has nothing whatsoever in common with the *Uncle Toms* that comprise her mother's generation, the willing and happy slaves of the male masters, the bootlickers who are now, for the most part, thirty years later, so alone, so warped by their years in chains that they are tiresome to everybody but each other. She feels deep sorrow for these old slaves, knocking around in their new apartments totally bewildered by their sudden freedom from husband and children, lost. She often feels lost. She does not know who she is; she has never had a nickname, she is not well-defined. She is here, sitting patiently in the back, waiting, waiting for me to recognize her and cut her off. For the longest time, I didn't even notice her. Where are the eleven other Judiths?

A friend's grandfather had fought in the Great War and suffered shell shock. After a while, he totally recovered, except that once in a while, on cold days, he would be out walking when he would see himself, in the distance, moving slowly towards him.

(1990)

Judith Thompson: Interview
by Judith Rudakoff

Judith Rudakoff: Is writing plays a compulsion? A battle? A joy?

Judith Thompson: The initial impulse is a joy.

JR: What about the rest of the process—is it a business or a vocation?

JT: Theatre is a vocation. If it was a business, I'd be the stupidest business-person in the world! It's just not lucrative. I suppose it might be if I'd write the kind of hit play that would be produced in all the huge regional theatres, the ones with thousands of seats. It's not that I don't think I could write that type of play: I just haven't. I have to be honest and follow through with my instincts when I'm writing and that's not the direction my instincts are taking me right now.

When I write, I'm like the Eskimo with a sculpture: chiselling away until I come to the jewel, the shape. It's hard, hard work and it's only in the refinement that I find the nuggets.

It's not like it was before I had children. Now, I have four hours a day where I go to the office that Tarragon has given me, and I write. And it becomes like automatic writing. Stuff just comes out! Some of it is garbage and through my learned knowledge of structure I do something with it.

JR: When we sat on a panel together at the Goethe Institute/Toronto Free Theatre German Theatre Symposium in 1987, someone asked you the question, "why do you write," and your answer affected me greatly. You said, "it's not a question of wanting to or needing to write: it just pours out like blood."

JT: Yes, it does. But it pours out *when I sit down to work*. In the past five years especially, since I've had children, the writing has had to become a job. It's how I make a living.

JR: Did you choose theatre, or did theatre pick you? Could your field have just as easily been short-story writing or poetry?

JT: The theatrical medium is where I'm happiest. It's what I breathe, what I know. I've been involved in theatre since I was very young. My mother was involved in theatre and I was in a play for her when I was eleven. For me, it was like being apprenticed to a trade.

I'm doing a lot of film-writing now, but that's a separate medium. Film-writing is like having a second trade. I'm just learning about it, and that's taking a lot of time.

Writing for live theatre is what I have an instinct for. You know you're good at something when your unconscious knowledge of it is far beyond your conscious knowledge of it. It's when I surprise myself that the piece works!

JR: What's the difference for you between writing for film and writing for theatre?

JT: The main difference is that in film I think with my eyes and dialogue is disposable. Dialogue is the essence of theatre.

JR: Urjo Kareda once said that one of the most extraordinary elements of your work is your ability to give audience members a moment during each performance when, individually, they will say to themselves: "How did she know that secret about me?" It's uncanny how you can reach into other people's unconscious, how you can get in past the civilized mask.

JT: I do believe in a collective unconscious. I believe that we can all relate to everything. Somewhere. Somehow. And then there's truth. The concept of truth is not limited to our society. The dream exists in other societies.

JR: Civilization imposes outside barriers on people, so that there's a certain person that we show to the world. Your plays explore people trying to find what's on the inside and access it, discovering that that inside is a difficult place to get to. Your characters seem to want to rip open their chests and let it all come out: sometimes they can't and sometimes they can.

JT: There's a difficult line between civilized and uncivilized in society. We have to keep the uncivilized part of ourselves under wraps: Plato was right. The old id, as Freud knew, has to be kept buried very deep. In murderers, the id is screaming.

When I write, my own conscious is very close to the surface. I look at it a lot and I spend a lot of the process getting to know myself, like psychoanalysts who learn their trade through being psychoanalysed themselves.

I was so far away from myself when I began in theatre that I don't think a word that came out of my mouth was true. Not a gesture. I do agree with Plato about keeping elements buried, but it's very important for us to keep in touch with what's going on inside. Once you're in your late twenties and thirties if you don't do serious work on who you are, if you don't acknowledge and meet fatality, then there is such damage that can be done. You have to really work. You have to think and work on yourself.

This begins to sound like I'm some kind of evangelist and I'm not. I'm more like an *idiot savant* at the first stage of the writing. I just try to get inside the characters and they become amalgamations of my relatives, my friends, my acquaintances. One person will say to me, "Dammit, I've always wanted to be

the centre," and these bells go off and it becomes the central speech of the play—
I sort of just take it. I take things that I've seen. Things from when I was little.
I'm like a magpie: I throw it all into the soup!

And then the play starts to develop its own structures and themes and it
says, "No. I don't want this part. It may be a brilliant little metaphor, but throw
it out! It's no good!" And I have to pick out all those things that don't belong.
And often, I end up taking out all the things with which I began the play.

But what's left after that stage is what's grown up underneath it. Like when
you put a band-aid on and suddenly the skin is grown over, the scab falls off and
there it is: there's the play. Because, you see, all my first ideas, the ones I discard,
were false—imposed—just me being clever.

The creation happens itself. I am somehow fortuitously plugged in. It all
comes through the typewriter! It's such hard, hard work after the first couple of
drafts, you know. With the first few drafts, everything does flow out, but then
it's a case of refinement, refinement and refinement, sometimes for years.

There are times when I think that the reason I am successful is that I work
really, really hard at it.

But I turn a lot of people off with my plays.

JR: There are a lot of people out there who feel something penetrating their
civilized shield, and they're not ready to be probed, the skin has grown too thick.
Those are the ones, it seems to me, at that moment when your work touches in,
that take off; they're the ones who walk out.

JT: They claim to have been bored. Or that they don't know people who talk like
my characters. And I have to respect them. Maybe for them it is boring. Maybe
they don't like the plays. It would be arrogant of me to say that it was them and
not me....

Let's go back to my shocking people—I am always very, very shocked
when people are shocked. The last thing I ever want to do is offend. I go out of
my way to please little old ladies. I would never offend them. I'm not the kind
of person who would say, "Well, to hell with you if you can't take a joke." I'm
really conservative that way. I like to please. I'm careful of people's feelings.
And yet, every time I write an adult play, it seems to become offensive to many
people....

I have these great aunts and I've spent hours and hours in their
apartments looking at old books. And I have a great sense of family. So it's so
horrible for me when I see these poor little old ladies—and I don't mean to be
condescending to them—getting upset and walking out. I feel terrible. Because
I guess I'm very naive when I write. It just doesn't occur to me that these
characters would offend anybody because they're people and I care about them.
And you just don't care about people because they're nice or they're pretty....

I would like to reach more people with my plays if I could, but what do I do? Do I compromise, or is there another way? *The Wizard of Oz* reaches more people and it penetrates into the collective unconscious and our need for home: maybe I'll write a *Wizard of Oz*! Actually, I have been thinking that maybe I'll write a children's play because that way I wouldn't feel the instinct to be offensive. I have children and I know what they can tolerate and cope with.

JR: Are people surprised when they see you for the first time?

JT: It's funny. I'll be at weddings or functions and the person sitting next to me will think I must be racy or radical and talk to me in a vulgar way because of my plays. I just turn away, disgusted. I'm really very conservative in many ways. My characters say these things—I don't. I don't use that language. Unless I'm forced to. And then I'll qualify it.

A lot of people expect green hair.

JR: How do you deal with these types of reactions?

JT: Maybe I try to counteract it by dressing particularly conservatively. Sometimes I really admire those people with the green hair and I wish that I could make a piece of art out of myself, but then I realize that I just don't want to intimidate people, to draw attention to myself. Because if I did that, then they wouldn't talk to me. I like people to be open with me. I think that there are times when I unconsciously play low-status so that people will be comfortable with me....

I do these things because I want to know about people. It took me years to learn to *listen*, rather than just wait till the other person finished talking. And I realized that there was a whole world of people out there saying things that I wanted to know. Now I listen and find out so much.

I have a real allegiance to the truth. About people. Some people say, "Well, diarrhoea is a fact of life, but we don't show that on stage..." That's the old argument: psychological truths are different. Physical truths are one thing, we understand and see them; we do not know about psychological truths. We hide them.

JR: In terms of the writing process, you also listen to your characters, don't you?

JT: I have a really low threshold of boredom. So I act out parts and then I know when sections are too long. I cut, cut, cut.

It's really the only way for me, the acting out. And still, I forget and I don't do it and then I make the same mistakes in everything I write, every time. I have to go the long way around every time.

For instance, in *I Am Yours* there was a male character I was having trouble with and I thought, "Well, why not inhabit him for a while?" and then I realized, suddenly, how everything should be. Just by feeling like that character, by being him in that situation: that's how I knew exactly how it should be.

JR: Can you give me an example of when you didn't inhabit the character, act him out, and where that led you?

JT: Cape Race in *White Biting Dog*. I don't think I fully inhabited him. I think he was half there. Or maybe he was there as a person but not … there's a real difference between character and characterization.

Character is what you do, your actions. It's truly who you are, especially in times of crisis. It's the choices that you make. Characterization is the person you present to the world.

With Cape, I just didn't get it. I didn't "go the distance."

You know, I suppose there's definitely an element of me in my characters. I don't know if that's just the part of me that taps into the collective unconscious, or if that's what makes me me.

It doesn't have to be true. Take Dee in *I Am Yours*, for example. I even heard people in the audience saying, "I understand she wrote this when she was pregnant and she was feeling very ambivalent…." Never. Not for a moment.

On the other hand, Dee is not a complete character. I've got to go back. She's complete as a character *inside*, but not outside. I need something to help people in, to make her more appealing.

JR: When people talk about your work, they often try to reason it out, to explain it. Does that annoy you?

JT: I love every take, every interpretation.

JR: Even the academics who suggest that the white dog is obviously God spelled backwards … ?

JT: I think it's wonderful. There have been academics who have written papers that have revealed things to me. I don't pretend to be the author in the sense of the Knowing Creator. Often academics will find wonderful parallels and they'll say, "The street sign was 'Redwing' and the colour of the sky was red" when I chose the name because I just liked the sound of "redwing." Or because I saw a street sign that day when I was walking home from the grocery shop that said "Redwing."…

JR: Are there other ways in which you work that are important to you?

JT: Unconsciously, there is some kind of structural working out that I'm not totally aware of. But it's there. I'm tremendously lucky that "it," that the images just happen for me. Sometimes when it doesn't work (for example, there'll be a song or something that doesn't fit), I'll consciously stop and say, "Well, there should be something in it about chickens." Or whatever.

There are times when I set out to write and I think, "Oh, sisters are interesting," and I'll write a monologue about pennies, and then one day I'll just sit down and write a plot outline, it'll just come. And I try not to think about it when I go home, because it's just too disturbing, and I close everything up and go home and fix dinner!

For me, the best things happen when I think. I get the chisel out and say, "Okay, crack the brain open." And I think, "Well, of course, *this* has to be *here*."

As playwrights, we do all this for years and years and years and then people see it in two hours and they don't get one hundredth of what's in there. That's one reason I do appreciate those academics: because at least they take the time to see the layers and layers that would really take ten or fifteen viewings to penetrate. One might ask, is it worth it to write something so dense because, after all, people are only likely to see it once, and plays are difficult to read?

It is. Because that way it penetrates in a subliminal way. People will live with those images for a long time.

JR: Do you ever have the urge to go back after a first production and rewrite for the second production?

JT: If *White Biting Dog* was ever done again I'd do a lot of rewrites and I'd do a lot of cutting. We staged a scene for the 1987 Toronto Arts Awards with Shirley Douglas and Stephen Ouimette as Lomia and Pascal, a break-up scene. And it was then that I realized that I had just overwritten it. The writing was too self-consciously lyrical. I was intoxicated with lyricism. The play doesn't need all those strong images piled one on top of the other. That's what I'm learning from the cinema. Less *is* more.

The poor audience: people who are trapped in the theatre and they have to listen to some writer who is just showing off, flexing her muscles…

JR: Do you think that playwrights should ever direct their own work?

JT: Writers should be able to direct their own works. They know the theatre. Essentially, I've directed all of mine. And I'm not a great director. I understand my plays, though. I understand them well and I'm pretty good with physicality, but I do stupid, terrible things with blocking. For instance, in NYC I had all three monologues at the same spot, till at the end the Artistic Director came by and said, "Judith, say, how about if we move them around?"

I understand everything about my plays. And I love it when someone has a better idea than I do. I love someone to come in and see things in a directorial way and turn it upside down, do wonderful things … it just hasn't happened yet.

It's not that the people who direct my plays haven't been good—because they have; it's just that perhaps their own visions were overwhelmed by mine. Because they had respect for my vision, they didn't allow their own to emerge.

Steven Bush did a wonderful production of *I Am Yours* in Ottawa in 1988. It was more visceral than Derek Goldby's premiere production at the Tarragon. Derek's production was problematic because it was really a co-direction with me. There were brilliant performances in it, but at the same time the actors felt stifled by us in a way.

There used to be a lot of new plays where the playwrights really didn't know what they were doing: they didn't know the theatrical medium, and they needed the actors desperately, to show them what the play was. I need the actor to play the piece, and to play it brilliantly, and to inhabit the work like Yehudi Menuhin inhabits a Bach piece. Menuhin is no less an artist because he doesn't write the notes.

I can't seem to convince actors that I have tremendous respect for their art, but that I don't need them to tell me who the character is. I know and I'm telling them. They can't say to me, "But this guy smokes." He does not smoke. I'm telling them. He comes from my unconscious and it would be sort of like them telling me that my mother wears wigs. She does not. I know. I feel like telling them, "You write your own play."

I do need them to bring their heart, their emotion, their experience and to play it. There's a million things for them to find and play within the borders of their art.

Now the second, third, fourth productions: they do what they like. But in the premiere production I think there must be a mandate to present the writer's play.

JR: Do your characters believe in anyone? Let's take Sandy in *The Crackwalker* as an example.

JT: Sandy believes that there's a right way to be and she's extremely Calvinist. She believes that the salt and pepper should be kept up in the second cupboard. She believes that when you butter toast, you butter to the edges. She believes that you have a cup of tea at ten o'clock. You don't wear mismatching socks, you wear matching gloves, you have your buttons done up, you have your clothes cleaned, you have your supper at five.

In other words, the quotidian is what saves her from the abyss.

She believes that if you buy everything you're taught and you live the way you are taught to live, you will be saved from the monster that's hovering around the periphery of civilization.

She's awfully surprised that she's not safe and her husband leaves. She keeps trying to observe these little laws and here are the monsters, yawning, right in her living room.

That scene where she's in bed with Theresa staying over and she goes out on the balcony and screams and screams and then comes back in and says, "It was nothing." Well, that's because it *can't* be anything. There are no monsters. I think maybe that's why we teach children about monsters: so that when they're eight we can turn around and tell them, "There are no monsters." And it's not till they're twenty-five that they realize, "Yes … there are…."

I am still really truly surprised when I find out that policemen are sometimes corrupt. Because I believed what I was told about them. Like Sandy. She really believed all those things and she's very kind. She accepts Theresa for what she is. She says, "No, you're not retarded, you're just a little slow." And once you describe someone, they're okay. Sandy's a big pigeon-holer. "She's a little slow, but she's got a warm heart." Then that's all right.

So she believes in civilization, that it can be maintained. If you learn how to make a new drink then that's an achievement—and it is. And it's something she's done. She believes that you can put on eyeliner a different way and it can change your life.

JR: How would you define "the abyss"?

JT: The abyss is death. It's what you don't know. It can be terrible conflict at, for example, work. I live such a smooth life: I've made sure of that. You see an abyss when you're falling, in that dream where you're falling and falling and there's no bottom.

JR: Emily Dickinson's concept of the abyss was death, and for years she'd go visit dying people. She wanted to see what happened after they went over the edge, into death.

JT: Everybody reads her poems at funerals. That wonderful poem about the "leagues out to sea, sweet intoxication." I want her poems to be read to me when I die: they're such a comfort. But do you think they're real? Do you think she ever found comfort watching all those people die?

JR: No. I don't think she did. That was the problem. What she did discover was a new definition of God: a non-Christian view of God as the "columnar self" spiralling ever inward to a point at the centre of the self.

JT: God is a newborn baby. Truly. You can really see God in a newborn baby. And it stays with them for a long time.

God is in every person—that's really hard to remember sometimes.

I do believe that God is in every one of my characters showing me herself. At little moments.

That's as scary as it is beautiful.

God is the innocence of a newborn baby; when people show that part of themselves, that eternal flame that's guarded; when they show that that's a moment of pure beauty, when they let you see it. Some people's flame seems to have gone right out….

Spontaneity—that's what we look for on stage. Bring on a dog or a baby and everyone's blown away. The search for that spontaneity is religious.

JR: Do you consider yourself or your characters optimistic?

JT: I think I'm very optimistic, yes. I think I'm not cynical or pessimistic at all— I should be more cynical than I am. Pony, in *White Biting Dog*, believes in the good in everybody. She's not stupid. Obviously, though, you become more cynical as you become more experienced.

JR: Or as you enter more into the real world. Do you find that the characters who are more rooted in reality depend more on reality and are less optimistic?

JT: If you have the good fortune to come from a good and loving home, you're encouraged and loved and get a lot of attention. Then you go into the world and people are nasty. I think that there is a sadistic impulse in everybody and that's where torture begins.

JR: Can you give me an example from the plays?

JT: Alan, in *The Crackwalker*, is tortured by his own mind, his own fears, the cauliflower. He's tortured by his lack of self esteem because he can never quite match up. He'll be feeling really good, and then somebody will be haughty to him because his coat has a stain on it. People won't treat him as an equal, can't get it through their heads that the person lying in the gutter is no different than they are at all. They are actually fooled by the hype that there is such a thing as "better."

JR: People often talk about your characters in terms of their social group....

JT: My characters just don't have a particular social group.

JR: Let's phrase that differently: do you think that your characters can escape their upbringing?

JT: My characters can't escape the effects of environment, because they'll always, always be with you. But just because your parents didn't read doesn't mean that you can't. Although you might be less likely to want to

JR: At the end of *The Crackwalker*, do you think that Sandy and Joe are going to change their lives? Will Calgary make a difference?

JT: No, Calgary to Joe and Sandy is like Moscow—pie in the sky. Joe will repeat his mistakes. It's very hard to change.

JR: Obviously your upbringing has had something to do with who you are and what comes out in your writing. How do you think living in Toronto for a good number of years and having children will affect the writing yet to come?

JT: Having children had a huge effect on my writing. I have become more in touch with myself and with wonder. It's just helped me. I've always been kind of a child myself so maybe having children has made me into more of an adult.

It's also helped me in the sense that with children around you, you can't be solipsistic.

JR: Do you take your children to see theatre?

JT: I do take my children to theatre. And when I was a child I always went.

JR: If you could bring a new audience into the theatre, who would you want to entice? What would you offer them?

JT: I want the people who go to hockey games at Maple Leaf Gardens to go to plays. I don't blame them for not going, it's generally very disappointing. To me, in any event. But we're all striving to make it better. We are all willing to admit that there are many disappointments, *but* there is this, somewhere in there, this golden egg, this moment we're all striving for, this moment of pure experience. What I call Truth. And when it *is* there....

I'm having an ongoing argument with a Marxist friend. Marxists all are very snide if you say you think there is such a thing as Truth. They don't believe that there's any such thing as a moment, say, in theatre or in any art that transcends time, culture, generation, place. They think it's all contextual. They believe that we are moved because we are taught to believe that, for example, mothers should love their babies. They think that everything is placed and understood within an historical context. They don't believe anyone can be free of that.

Now, if that's true then I might as well throw all my stuff in the garbage and go home.

And I just find it enraging. How could it be true? Where does that leave the Grimms' fairy tales? My daughter is moved by them. They're timeless. And that sense of timelessness, that truth: that's what we're all striving for.

I keep telling my Marxist friends that context does help to bring the audience into the moment; it does help to lead them there. If you recognize yourself, then you're more likely to identify a little bit. Some people say, "Oh, Judith, your dialogue is so great." Well, dialogue is nothing, it's just an ear, it's just dressing to help people into the moment.

Actors always say, "Oh, I like your words." Well, it's the third, fourth, fifth thing down the line for me if we're talking about what makes a play work. Its those moments, those timeless moments that make the difference—the dreaded word: Truth.

When there is Truth in a play, when one of those moments happens, in any play, no matter how messy its structure is, or how flawed its thinking is, then I'll praise it to the sky.

JR: Is there an artist, either of our time or not, who writes with this truth? Who has these moments?

JT: Howard Brenton. Lawrence Jeffery. Sally Clark. Joan MacLeod. Colleen Murphy.

I was, of course, also influenced by Tennessee Williams, Edward Albee, Mickey Mouse, "My Favourite Martian," "Mr. Ed" the Talking Horse—it's true! Really. Because we grew up watching them everyday on television. Ours was a typical late-fifties, early sixties household, so I can't deny it: I must have been heavily influenced by all that pap. Not that Mickey Mouse is pap!

Mickey Mouse: why do we, as children, respond to that little mouse! Truth, again.

And there's also great Truth in the Grimms' fairy tales. They influenced me greatly. Anyone who looks closely at my work can see that. But again, we're talking about tapping into a collective unconscious. They do, and I hope when my plays are working they do the same kind of thing. I think the Grimms' fairy tales gave me the courage. I didn't used to think you needed courage! People used to say, "Oh Judith, you're so brave," and I'd think, "Brave, you don't have to be brave to have a character killing a baby on stage. That's just what the character does. That's what happened." And the Grimms' fairy tales are *worse* than anything I write! Far worse.

JR: What's your favourite fairy tale?

JT: I don't know which my favourite is. They're all the same tale, in a way. There are actually about three tales.

And the major recurring character in most of them is the Bad Mother, the Wicked Stepmother. I think it must be little girls' Electra conflict coming out: Freud was right.

I am a devoted Freudian in some ways. I've read all his work. I went through all of it in about a year and a half and audited a course on him when I was on a Canada Council B-Grant. He does have that fairy-tale desire to make everything fit into his scheme. It doesn't.

On the other hand, in fairy tales you also have the Blue Fairy and the Fairy Godmother, because the kids, the daughters, of course, do love their mothers and need them.

Did these authors know this? I doubt it. In fact, I never understand what I write a lot of the time. I'm just amazed at it myself.

JR: Have you noticed that in your plays, most of the time, if you have a mother, then you give her a son?

JT: I guess I do have mothers and sons in my plays. I wonder why I do that....

JR: Well, let's take one of the less obvious mother-son relationships: Theresa and her son in *The Crackwalker*.

JT: When I was working as an Adult Protective Service Worker, I met a couple who had had a son and the father had killed him.

That was the kernel of that story, of those characters.

You know, maybe I would have done better to make Cape a woman....

Of course, the obvious answer as to why I write about mothers and sons is that I was brought up a Catholic and there's one big mother-son relationship!

I had been thinking, before writing *White Biting Dog*, about manipulative people, sociopathic people and why they are the way they are. I know a few and by coincidence they all happen to be male. Men have a different sense of what power is than women do.

I looked at a religious card the other day and it said, "He has risen" and I thought—can you imagine growing up with, "She has risen"? Can you imagine the difference that would have made to who you are? She has risen.

JR: Often your characters seek shelter or draw strength from the women in your plays, even if their situations are little better.

JT: Yes, people do come to the women for strength. To the mother in them. Yes, you're right, Sandy acts that way too. Sandy fixes everything. Theresa fixes Alan. Pony, Lomia do. Not in *I Am Yours*, though. In that play Mac was the only fixer.

It startles me when my plays come out because I never think they are a map of my unconscious. I really do believe that they are a map of the collective unconscious.

JR: Do you work with the designers of your productions? Do you see a play in the same way that you hear it?

JT: I feel sorry for whoever designs my plays: they're so filled with voices in the dark. Not so much any more. And I do have some, a handful, of strong visual images for each play.

In *I Am Yours*, all the designers could really do is make an acting machine, so that with all the short scenes it wouldn't be clunky. Jim Plaxton did a nice job. Cathy Norman did a lovely job in Ottawa and actually made the environment quite pretty. There was less distance for them to travel. Fatter and wider. Beautiful. It really worked.

I tend to say things to designers like, "I see it sparkling." You know, luralex sets! I'm really developing that visual side of myself because I'm working more in films. I'm thinking visually and it's going to help my next play.

JR: There have been some strong visual images in previous productions, for example the big drainpipe centre stage in the premiere production of *The Crackwalker* at Toronto Workshop Productions.

JT: The big drainpipe in *The Crackwalker*. I don't know if I'd like that again. I loved it then. In a way I don't like it because I hate the notion that *The Crackwalker* is about the underbelly of society.

They're not that horrible. They're not that different from anybody. It's infuriating.

Well, they're not the wealthy, privileged class—that's true. But how is Sandy different from most of the women in the audience? A little less education maybe....

And all of us have a little of Theresa in us: the innocent, the child who wants to be protected and have no responsibility.

And Joe. It doesn't matter what class the man is from. There are a lot of Joes everywhere. And Joe is not stupid. None of them are. Even Alan isn't stupid, just emotionally troubled. In fact, he's probably the brightest. But that's how people make themselves comfortable, by saying, "Oh that play is not about me, it's about the underbelly."

The underbelly to me would be like, I don't know, the mob, drugs. Underbelly in the sense that it goes on all around us and we don't know.

JR: Are you protective or selfish of any aspect of the work? Either in the process or the developing of characters or during the rehearsal period?

JT: Well, I cut a lot on my own. I love to take the red pencil and cut. But in the rehearsals for *I Am Yours*, Derek Goldby cottoned on to me early on and told the actors, "Don't ever ask Judith to cut a line or she'll never cut that one."

Actors get quite angry sometimes when I cut, they think I'm cutting *them* out. I'm not. I'm just cutting the play. But if anybody tries to make me cut a line I never will. It's stupid and childish and I can't help it.

I'm very protective of Truth. There's that word again. And when I know that a character wouldn't do or say something or has to say something, then wild horsemen couldn't make me change it. I just won't. That's the only thing I'm strong about. I'm a wimp in every other way. But when it comes to the work and what's right or wrong, nothing can persuade me. Because I know it in my bones.

JR: What's the strangest production of one of your plays that you've either seen or heard about?

JT: It was strange to hear the Chicago production of *The Crackwalker* in thick Chicago accents, because I thought of it as so Southern Ontario. But of course that doesn't matter. It was strange to me that there was a production of it translated into Hebrew in Tel Aviv. Talk about no context. That's one for our side. Here are people living in a war-torn country. What are they going to care about these characters on welfare in a peaceful country getting enough to eat and not dying, not getting shot? So what's the problem? What's to worry about? That's what I would have thought would be the reaction. But they related to it tremendously.

JR: Do you consider yourself either a Canadian playwright of a feminist writer? Is there a difference in perspective that comes with either of those titles?

JT: Well, according to the Marxists, there must be! I suppose it depends on how different you think essence of male is from essence of female

In terms of male or female perspective, I suppose that a lot of people might say that my writing is very male. It's full of rage and a lot of women have had that stamped out of them. I think that's why there are fewer women writers. And I notice that when we audition actors, many women have trouble with real, pure rage. It's seen as masculine territory. Or maybe it is masculine and I'm just butch! Rage isn't nice. It's one of the seven deadly sins. I don't get angry much, really. I'm not an angry person, but I could get angry. But there's a lot of that kind of feeling in my plays and I think that's why they're so offensive to so many people. I'm glad I started out so excessive because by my late middle age I'll just be "kind of strong," whereas other people who started out subtle just go to mush. Real Pablum.

JR: Has it been harder for you to get produced in Canada because you are a woman writer?

JT: It's probably been easier for me being a woman playwright because many theatres like to say they're producing women's plays. What's tough for me is the rehearsal period. I've been referred to as a ball-breaker and there have been rumours that directors hated me. Well, I just speak my mind, the Truth. If I was a guy, I'd just be a man saying his piece.

I don't consciously address feminist issues. Ever. But I might say to myself, "When I was growing up, I liked men who guided me, who took the wheel." My girl friends and I would talk and say that we couldn't stand it when a male said, "May I kiss you?" How wimpy and awful. And this was terrible. Where did this come from? And because it was true of me I would think it was true of a lot of women.

And then I want to know why. So I create a character who goes to the extreme of masochism. And I'm certain that a lot of feminists would take issue with that and say that you are not to portray a masochistic female, because that's perpetuating a notion that's incorrect. To that I would say, no, it's examining an issue that's true, and until you examine what is, what exists, you can't do anything about it. Until you open up the wound and find that bullet and say, "Yup, the bullet is there," you can't get it out. If you pretend the bullet isn't there, it's going to stay there and it's going to erode the whole body, the whole system.

You've just got to tell the truth and leave it at that. The horrible Truth.

Luckily, I'm not apolitical, but I try not to concern myself too much with politics. I mean, I vote NDP but I can't be political because it would ruin the work. To be political is to bend the Truth. I can be a recorder of the Truth.

JR: Can you define "Grace" as opposed to "Truth"?

JT: Truth is simply what is. It happens to you through not doing anything. For example, you feel hatred although you've been pretending to feel love. Or you feel the impulse to do something. That's Truth.

Grace is something you achieve. Through work. And Grace is something you have to work and work at. It happens through penitence, through sight. Through seeing who you are and changing things. You achieve it through humility.

JR: You've called *White Biting Dog* a play about Grace. Can you be more specific about that?

JT: Pony achieves Grace because she understands when she falls in "love" that something has possessed her, taken her over, and that that something can wipe out all her moral character.

In other words, she knows that for this love, if he asked her to kill someone, or never to see her family again, she would comply. Because she was possessed by this infatuation, this love, she decided that it wasn't worth the anguish and that she would have to kill herself in order to conquer this possession. If you have a child murderer, the only decent thing he can do is kill himself. Obviously, he's possessed. I don't know how many people walk around with this urge and don't do anything about it. Maybe many, maybe none. Radical evil, once it enters you, seems to be stronger than most human beings.

Anyhow, Pony had the strength to conquer that radical evil. Now I'm certainly not advocating suicide. This is all in the abstract, metaphor. But I am talking about killing the radical evil, conquering a it at extreme risk to yourself. That's why I had to have it as a suicide in the play. But there's a side to people and to my character that would rather be all alone than be with a person who would cause you to do harm to others. Working through that can bring you to Grace. It's that difficult.

The old man in *White Biting Dog* also achieves Grace, also at the expense of his own happiness. Lomia and Cape, on the other hand, are amoral human beings who didn't even take the first step. You have to work and work and pray.

And that's what I was talking about at the beginning of this interview. You can't just get up out of bed, go to work, come home. As a writer, this is what I'm always thinking about: how we really have to do this work on ourselves. And that's why I think theatre can be very important. It's urgent that people see good theatre with those moments I call Truth. It will help them do the type of thinking I'm talking about. It will prevent those black holes of people who are fifty-five and walking around and not a word they say is sincere and you can't believe it. They don't listen. They have no Truth. Or Grace.

(1990)

An Interview with Judith Thompson
by Eleanor Wachtel

Eleanor Wachtel: Your work is filled with … I don't know if I should say this … horrifying moments, moments of confession, revelation and emotional crisis. It doesn't matter whether you're writing about yuppies or working-class people or characters who are self-aware or characters who are crazy. Why do you feel drawn to this dark side of the psyche?

Judith Thompson: It's not so much that I'm drawn to the dark side as that I'm interested in the invisible side of human beings. I think that's what theatre should do, is show us what is invisible and covered up with piles of everydayness and everyday life.

EW: But what's invisible tends to be … not a pretty picture. What's kept hidden seems to be maybe hidden for a reason.

JT: I don't know that it's not pretty. For instance you look at the sugar scene [in *Lion in the Streets*], when the working-class caregiver expresses her rage towards the "yuppie" parents. They would be unaware that they had deeply insulted her by saying that they think it's disgusting that she gives their children yogurt with honey in it—

EW: What you're calling the sugar scene is the scene where there is the mother of a child at the daycare centre who is upset because she doesn't want her children to be given any sugar at all and the caregiver has taken the kids out for donuts, right?

JT: That's right, one time.

EW: And eventually the caregiver vents her rage.

JT: She tells them what she thinks of them and how deeply insulting and classist the whole thing is. It's a kind of catharsis. It's what we all want to do in some situations at some time and haven't been able to do because we have to hang on to our job or keep our reputation intact, or whatever. That's what I always love to do in the theatre, to give us a chance to do what we want to do, through the characters.

EW: I was going to say that that's not the most grotesque scene of the undersides or the invisibles that is shown! There is the scene with Isobel, who's probably dead herself, coming on and shooting all the parents.

JT: That's right! She's sort of enacting Rhonda the caregiver's deepest wishes at that moment. I guess what I'm exploring there is the source of that kind of homicidal rage. I'm not saying it's ever justified in any way, but we have to look at the source, in order to explore it at all. Often, I think it comes from a perceived persecution; why do certain individuals feel they're being persecuted? Where does that come from? They might blame it on someone who's altogether innocent—they do—completely innocent.

EW: I think virtually every scene—in, for example, your newest play, *Lion in the Streets*—uncovers, or makes visible this invisible side. But it uncovers something pretty disturbing.

JT: Yes. Well, I suppose it's Isobel's journey-odyssey through an ordinary neighbourhood, which is becoming gentrified, so we get a little bit of everything—rooming house, basement apartment, renovated Victorian house— and she descends into the underworld of these lives, what we don't see. You're walking down the street and you see lights and houses and you peek through and see a television or a little dinner party going on, but what's happening really, inside each life?

EW: What I'm interested in is why you want to walk through the underworld of all these lives?

JT: Well, because it's theatrical, it's what's true, and it's like the purpose the church used to serve: for an hour a week we would confront our spirits, what was really happening. In the theatre I think what one must do is confront the truth, confront the emotional truth of our lives, which is mired in the swamp of minutiae, everyday minutiae. Maybe it has to be that way, because we couldn't confront it every day. But I think the theatre must. I'm not interested in theatre that doesn't.

EW: You once said that even ordinary conversation seems extraordinary on the stage.

JT: That's right. One critic said that a lot of these things couldn't happen, but yes, they definitely could, and we could all come up with ten newspaper accounts of things like that that have happened. The only thing that couldn't happen— although maybe it could!—is that someone could come back from the dead. But who knows!

EW: Your first play, *The Crackwalker*, which you wrote ten years ago, and which is currently being remounted at the Tarragon Theatre, is set in a very harsh world of poverty and abuse. You don't romanticize or sanitize these lives or that world. Is it risky for you, brought up in a basically upper middle-class background? Is it risky for you to cross class lines, to try to get into that world?

JT: I suppose presumptuous, in a way, although I really feel that I had connected with the people that I wrote about, in *The Crackwalker*, when I worked as an assistant to an Adult Protective Service worker. I became quite close to them—

this was for the Ministry in Kingston, and these people were supposedly permanently unemployable. When I wrote it, it wasn't about the class thing so much as about these human beings.

EW: I wonder if you have to think about whether you're being exploitive or if you have to think that—on the other extreme—you're humanizing these people, giving them a voice—do you sort of walk between those two kinds of lines?

JT: I don't know. Sure, I felt, how can I represent these people? But I guess these people, to some extent, must reside within me, just in the way they reside within you and in all of us. I think that's kind of my unconscious point: we do share a collective unconscious and we have as much in common with Alan, the so-called deranged fellow in *The Crackwalker*—who goes right off the edge—as you and I have with each other, really. We just have to look beyond his choice of language—the way he expresses himself, the way he lives—and into his soul, and there's really no difference. That's why I'm kind of dismayed when the press approaches and says this is the underbelly, these people are very foreign to us. In my mind these people are us, in those circumstances.

EW: I can go along with that, up to a point. We want what Alan wants, Alan wants what we all want. We want love, we want some sort of family, or some sort of connection to each other. He wants that, but then he takes it to a place…. He ends up murdering, killing his baby.

JT: Yes, because he's been so weakened by all the forces acting upon him, including internal forces. It's like the notion that it's only the Germans in 1944 who made the holocaust. They were just, needless to say, people like us—that's what's truly horrifying to me. That's what I can't get out of my head. We're living in a pathological state of denial, as a society, as a culture, and we have to stop it right now. Just having to walk past homeless people, having to—just deny, deny, deny.

EW: What happens if you don't?

JT: I think you can barely put one foot in front of the other. Especially if you allow yourself to try and imagine, try and experience the horror…. I almost felt it was my duty to experience the fear that people have had to experience. I think ultimately that's good for us. Ultimately, as a culture, we can stop these things if we experience them, if we have to go through what other people have to go through.

EW: It's a bit like the idea of the scapegoat. It's like you have chosen to sensitize yourself or be so responsive to all the evil vibrations that are out there.

JT: I have—and it's not to say I'm this noble Joan of Arc. It's like they forgot to nail in the storm windows in my head! But it's true, sometimes I find it totally unbearable.

EW: I want to go back to these moments of crisis in your characters, for a moment, where they lose themselves, or they go over the top, or something bizarre is exposed. You once said that your own creative process could possibly be linked to your experience of epilepsy, something that first affected you as a child.

JT: I don't know, that's just a shot in the dark, but I thought maybe the reason I can draw on these things fairly easily—it's not difficult for me. My little metaphor about the storm windows is that something's kind of loose. I've been very fortunate, I've had very mild epilepsy—three to four attacks in my whole life—the last one being six years ago. But I sometimes think the firing goes on— the electrical storms they talk about—is what results in this gush of language that I'll stand back from after I've written it and say wow, where did that come from? Not to be immodest but I sometimes don't know myself how I could put it together with the emotions and everything that's going on. I don't know if it's a musical instinct….

EW: You described your epilepsy in a story you wrote for radio. In that piece you talk about epilepsy as a kind of evil animal or monster, with a lot of different faces. In some of your plays there are characters who feel devoured by animals or different kinds of things that are eating them up. Are these the same animals, these monsters, are they related?

JT: I think they are. It's probably just radical evil. And epilepsy is just something organically going wrong, obviously, but it feels like an outside force. I really understand why, in ancient times, they thought this was possession. Maybe it is!

EW: The notion of radical evil—it sounds so absolute.

JT: We've always been aware of it, they created the notion of Lucifer. Some people believe there is a Lucifer. And the notion of God. But they're inside us, and that war is going on inside us all the time. I think until we're aware of it, it's much harder to beat.

EW: Do you feel that? Do you feel you have God and the Devil inside, warring in you?

JT: In me, not so much—because I have been civilized. And I don't have evil impulses. But I think each character in my play is a sort of microcosm for the whole culture, because there is evil and good warring in the culture at all times. And I do think it's in every human being.

EW: Is this the Catholic in you?

JT: Probably! But don't you think it's true? We are animals, and that's what we try to persuade ourselves that we're not. There's a sort of mass delusion that we're not. A lot of our behaviour is almost biologically determined. You see that with a baby. With my baby, I'm just observing this. She's in a great mood, at some hours of the day, because everything digestively is going well. It's not really situational. It's biological.

EW: The body is very present in your work. The characters talk about bodily functions. They're very close to their bodies: they grow tumours, they bear children. Why do you think the work is so focused on the physical?

JT: I don't think it's any more focused on the physical than the emotional or the spiritual. I guess it's because I let each character speak. If we dive into any individual's inside or interior, we're going to find a lot of thinking about the body, unless you have these strange people who don't live in their bodies. There you get a really peculiar individual.

EW: Some of your characters are physically reduced to the level of animals, or they're trapped inside their bodies. There's a character, in *Lion in the Streets*, who has cerebral palsy—she's trapped in a wheelchair. She describes these vivid, erotic encounters that she may or may not actually be having, and she becomes almost a monster figure. She threatens to swallow up the reporter who comes to see her and who's very exploitive.

JT: Yeah: "I'll open my jaws and swallow—you will spend the rest of eternity in my body, and ohhhh, time goes slow!"

EW: Very creepy!

JT: That's right. She's just got the mind, and she's stuck, imprisoned.

EW: When one watches this omnivorous almost-monster, are you thinking there is some kind of monster that needs to be heard or recognized or unleashed?

JT: I don't find her a monster at all. I think she's a lot of fun, Scarlett. She's just enraged at what she's seen this journalist do. She suddenly realizes that she's been treated as an object, as a thing. So she is telling the journalist that she will go to hell for this.

EW: It's a very personalized hell. She's not just sent off to hell somewhere below, she's sent to hell somewhere *within*.

JT: "I am your nightmare, baby, I'm your worst nightmare, and you're going to be me, for having hated me."

EW: There are a number of images of possession in your plays. In *Lion in the Streets*, a character accuses an old schoolmate of holding his memory. Do you think other people, or past experiences, become part of us in ways that we don't necessarily acknowledge or that they possess us?

JT: Absolutely. And form us, too. It's like a piece of a puzzle, but a puzzle glued with cement. Once this experience—like the betrayal of Rodney by Michael— once it's in the puzzle, it's there. And it bleeds into all the other pieces. There's nothing he can do but worry it. He can't resolve it. That's why this is really a fantasy of Michael coming in and them having this encounter and him cutting Michael's throat—it doesn't really happen.

EW: These are two adults and they're recalling when they used to play chess together as school kids.

JT: That's right. But it's really only Rodney, you see. He just imagines Michael comes in, because he needs to play it out. I got that idea from my daughter—she once had a toy. We had to hurry and cross the street and she dropped it. A sports car came whizzing along and ran over it, flattened it. She was extremely traumatized by this and asked me to tell her the story over and over and over. Finally, after I'd told her day after day for a week, two weeks, then she would tell it, very unemotionally, but she'd tell it and she was fine about it.

EW: Children do figure a lot in your work. This was even before you became a mother of three—in rapid succession. Characters fight over children, over babies…. There's a baby that's kidnapped in *I Am Yours*, there's a baby that's murdered in *The Crackwalker*.

JT: Children are a huge part of ourselves. They're the beautiful, pure god in us. I felt, when I first had a baby, that I saw the face of God. If there is a God, that's what the meaning of it is. Complete purity. Children move me, and there's the child in all of us and how we try to beat it down and make it cower, or how it takes over in a terrible way, too—the terrible tyrant it can be.

EW: I think some of the invisible parts of characters that are given vent in *Lion in the Streets* are childlike: that pure emotion, that pure rage, that childlike part of ourselves.

JT: That's right. And we have to temper it, of course, and civilize it, but I think we also lose a lot of the wondrous purity at the same time.

EW: But that's not the side of the characters that you focus on. The wondrous purity.

JT: Oh, I think I do! Just think about Joanne's speech about Ophelia. She's dying of lung cancer and she's fantasizing about something that to her is extremely precious and beautiful. All of them have something they find precious and beautiful. Isobel loves Trans Ams, and she loves being invisible.

EW: Isobel is the young, dead Portuguese girl who winds her way through *Lion in the Streets*.

JT: That's right. She makes connections with each person who's suffering some kind of spiritual death or sickness.

EW: You do have what is almost, for you, a happy ending.

JT: It is. It's very hopeful. It's Isobel saying, "I want you all to have your life." It's the triumph of the spirit. I realized I have to be true to what I believe in, and I do—

EW: Believe in happy endings?

JT: Not happy endings—well, I believe that the spirit can triumph. We don't have to be walked over. It's like sticks and stones can break your bones but names can never … our bones can be broken but our selves, our souls, are much stronger than any destructor. It's saying to the evil forces, There's more, don't think you've got us. Don't think you've had any victory. I really sound like I live in a comic-book world.

EW: It's quite amazing! You want to be in touch and provide a forum, or expose, or whatever, all the evil that we spend our lives denying, in order to function. But at the other end of it you also want, and do, seem to feel hopeful.

JT: I really do. It's acknowledging that, yes, it's a jungle out there, there's a war, but we have our wonderful spirits and great strength, and yes, we have the Force—it's like "Star Wars:" we have the Force. And that's what Isobel's about, finding that Force in yourself and using it.

(1991)

Offending Your Audience

by Judith Thompson

What follows is selected from comments made at a panel discussion, moderated by Sky Gilbert, that took place in Toronto in February 1992 as part of Buddies in Bad Times' Rhubarb! Festival.

I've heard that all of my plays have offended a lot of people, and I'm not pretending a *naivete* but I am always surprised because I don't think I have any such intentions when I write.

Hoards of people left *The Crackwalker* and they always use the excuse of the language, but I never believed this excuse because in some of the subsequent plays, in scenes in which the language was tame, people were equally offended. They were so offended that they wanted not only to hate the plays but hate me. I was invited once to a faculty women's lunch and all of their husbands had cancelled their subscriptions to the Tarragon Theatre because of *White Biting Dog*. So I did a little middle-class shuffle, and then they really liked me and wanted their husbands to like me and get their subscriptions back. If I was a nice girl who'd written this terrible play, then it was okay. As if it was a sickness that just came out of me. When I explained it to them, they seemed to want to understand.

On the way here, I was thinking about what being offended means. In my case, I hope it is not to be alienated and turned away forever but more to be turned deeply red. It's the sensation when you're in a room with a group of people, and you're thinking something secret or private, and someone exposes it, saying "I know what you're thinking; you're thinking this."

Our whole society is founded on denial. Denial of murdering the Native people, denial of oppressing women. Everything we do. Once secrets are exposed, whatever it is—and people hate to turn red and be exposed—then they will hate you for it.

I try to let the characters write themselves and what they're saying is what they're saying. It wouldn't occur to me that something is offensive so a character can't say it.

I don't want to be condescending to people who are offended, so I want also to say that I've been offended when something is trivialized, like a half-dressed girl to get you to buy a car. Or in a feminist cabaret one year I left during a skit about abortion. A performer had a fake fetus that she was making talk, saying things like "I'm really a person" and stuff. I'm pro-choice and I've had an abortion, but to trivialize the issue like that just made me want to leave.

(1992)

Why Should a Playwright Direct Her Own Play?

by Judith Thompson

"I can feel it, rampaging through me. I have no strength against it. She has loosed it with her doubt, her loss of faith." These lines, taken from my adaptation of Ibsen's *Hedda Gabler*, which I directed at the Shaw Festival this summer,[1] baffled the actor who was being paid to say them. From the first day of rehearsals this actor had enormous hostility towards the adaptation, viewing it as a monstrous distortion of Ibsen's play, which he seemed to think was perfectly rendered by the existing English translations. Along with one or two others in the cast, he regarded the clumsy, wooden and decidedly unpoetic extant English translations as gospel. However, up until this point he had, albeit reluctantly, walked through my adaptation in rehearsals and tried to "make it work," as I had been fairly obliging, reinstating many lines I had, perhaps over-zealously, cut, and patiently explaining how I had arrived at each word or phrase that differed from the other translations. But today was different. He would not enter into this pivotal moment of the play; instead, he glared at me and declared the speech unactable. He said that it made no sense at all, and that he was not interested in a "wash of emotion." He emitted fumes of hatred into the rehearsal room, and I began to find breathing difficult. I tried to help him with the moment, presenting him with several strong metaphors, all of which he refused to hear: "No, no, *no, no*! It doesn't make sense." Finally, at breaking point, I told him that I had the perfect analogy. I, like Lövborg, could feel a "beast rampaging through me" because of his (the actor's) lack of faith in me and my adaptation. In fact, what I felt like doing was putting my head and his through the glass doors. The actor had been in a squatting position, staring at the floor while I spoke. When I finished, he remained frozen in that position for a full ten minutes, refusing to answer the stage manager's queries about his well-being. Inside, I shattered. This rehearsal process was the most painful and sickening one I have ever been through, and although the production was wonderful, and very well received, I doubt I will ever recover from the emotional trauma of directing it.

I am not a director. Personal politics are anathema to me, and, I think, very damaging to me as an artist and a human being. I am not a director. Why did I do it? Aside from wanting the chance to be "on site" in order to get the text right, I thought that I would find relief from the isolation of writing, but I found myself more alone than ever, like the kings of old, the lonely absolute monarchs, incarcerated by the throne. The director is a kind of dictator, a boss, and everybody, on some level, hates her boss. I always did. But one cannot solve this problem by throwing off the mantle of authority and declaring oneself a collaborator with a watchful eye, because most actors seem to have been habituated to expect a traditionally male kind of authority figure, a bearded man who knows the play better than any of them, who has the answers to all their questions and who, preferably, speaks with a British accent. They want a conqueror, someone who will take their natural resources and build a splendid and fruitful machine. They do not want someone who is groping in the dark without a sword, searching for the play. No! They want a *man* who will show them the light, so that they can crawl out of their chaos and barbarism, their darkness. The director must have a grand design that the primitives cannot see. Surely this need of theirs is a perfect example of a hunchbacked colonial mentality, and I feel most uncomfortable wearing Columbus's clothing. I, as a writer, never see a grand design. I am a mole, burrowing underground, bumping into the play. I can understand why actors might be uncomfortable with that—who wants a blind taxi driver? But I cannot play "Dad." I will not give pep talks before the first run-through, or flatter wilting egos, or scold lazy memories; that is what one does for children, not adult professionals!

But. In spite of all these democratic convictions, I cannot bear to have a tenth of a second on stage that I do not feel is right, and I have lots of ideas about exactly how a character's hands should spread above her head, and how another must never smile or cock her head, and on and on. And when an actor tells me that he/she feels something in "the back of my knees," my feeling is that *my* feeling in the back of my knees is more right than theirs. But do I know what is right because I am the playwright or the director? As the playwright, I might feel threatened if an actor knew more about my character than I do (although, when that happened, with Stephen Ouimette playing a role,[2] I was thrilled, humbled and awed). As the director, I feel that everything must be part of my "vision" or the whole thing will fall apart. I also fear that if I direct too much my "playwright cells" might re-arrange themselves into those befitting a dictator, and then I wouldn't be able to write another play. I don't know; it's a conundrum. I like to direct my own premières because I like to discover what, in fact, my vision is. I also like to have a direct line to the actors in order to constantly improve the text, without having to wait until the director has gone to the bathroom. In the past I have found that with a director between me and the actors I have compromised the text for the sake of keeping peace, and I will never let that happen again.

I believe that playwrights must understand and use their power once again. In the film world, the writer has been pretty well obliterated by the director, and I can see this movement in the theatre as well. This development is, of course, a clear reflection of a deeply patriarchal society feeling threatened by all that is female and baring its teeth. The writer, I believe, is a female force—a force of voice, music, emotion. The writer's words gush out of the mouths of the actors and inside the listeners, nestling and growing and swirling around. The writer gives birth to the work and the director, like society, shapes the newborn, making it a supposedly coherent, hard-hitting and palatable creature with *his* stamp on it.

Why did I always choose male directors? I suppose I was always looking for father figures. My three-year-old, Elias, asked me the other day, "How did we *get* in your tummy?" and when I told him that Daddy, in a way, put him there, he smiled knowingly and said, "Daddy can do anything." Just like directors, the omnipotent gods who shape the inchoate creation of the witless vessel.

All playwrights should direct their own work at some time, if only to fully experience the dramatic text. To direct your own play is to feel more in control of it, to feel like a muscular, thinking artist, and not an *idiot savant*, or a mere "wordsmith," as I was called by my first male director. To direct your own play is to have the *freedom* to express your feeling about the play, a freedom which can be cruelly taken from the writer by threatened directors. For example, I experienced one writer-director relationship for which the word "colonized" is very gentle, indeed. I was the Incas and he was Spain. It all started at a preliminary meeting at my house. He seemed edgy, and he avoided my eyes. When I handed him a rewrite of a monologue, explaining that I was not a great typist, he tore it up and then threw the entire bound script at me full force, yelling at me. I screamed the high-pitched squeal of a six-year-old, and repeated "Get out of my house" like a mantra. He put his hand on my head, said that I was "a very emotional girl, yes?" and then told me to sit on the couch and listen to what he had to say. Being a well-trained girl, I sat on the couch and stared out the window, tears streaming down my face. He paced up and down my tiny living-room, excoriating me and everyone else in Canadian theatre. "Would you like to know what I think of *Canadian theatre?!*" The word "mediocre" flew across the room many times. He told me that the only reason that he agreed to direct my play is that it is mildly interesting. Then, he pointed his finger at me and yelled, "If you ever dare say one word to the actors, *I will kill you. I will kill you, do you understand? I will kill you!!*"

Once rehearsals began it became clear that he was bewildered by the play. He was totally dependent upon me, and soon resorted to sending the actors out of the room after every scene, and then turning to me. I would tell him how the scene should be done and then he would bring the actors back and repeat to them verbatim what I had said. He forbade me to have lunch with one of my dearest friends who was acting in the play because he thought we were plotting against him. He would scream at the actors about anything at all—the atmosphere was unbearable.

Why had I let the collaboration continue after the dreadful episode at my house? I guess that I felt it was inevitable, and I was unconsciously relieved to be put in the position of an obedient child, a "good girl." And being yelled at, well, I guess I somehow thought it was punishment I deserved. I should, of course, have directed that production myself. I had a wonderful experience directing my most recent play, *Lion in the Streets*.[3] It was an almost perfect process. But I wouldn't particularly want to direct it again. I've got it *right* now—the text is right. Now

I want to see what other directors can do, such as the brilliant Claude Poissant in Montreal, who did such an astonishing production of *I Am Yours*, or *Je suis à toi*, and who is opening the French version of *Lion in the Streets* as I write. [4] I am humbled and delighted when a director like Claude Poissant or Stephen Bush tramples into my fragile dream with big muddy boots and leaves it the same, but at the same time utterly changed and strange. I believe that all playwrights should direct each of their works once, speaking to the actors *ex cathedra* so that they can see their own work, or prayer, in a clear light.

(1992)

Notes

[1] Court House Theatre, Niagara-on-the-Lake, 30 July–22 September 1991.

[2] Pascal in the first production of *White Biting Dog*, directed by Bill Glassco, Tarragon Theatre, Toronto, January 1984.

[3] First produced at the third biennial du Maurier World Stage Festival at Toronto's Harbourfront, 2–16 June 1990. Thompson's production also ran at the Tarragon Theatre, 30 October–9 December 1990.

[4] *Lion dans les rues*, trans. Robert Vezina, Théâtre de Quat' Sous, Montreal, 16 September–12 October 1991.

Computers Keep Your Office Tidier

by Ric Knowles

The following interview was published as part of a special issue of Canadian Theatre Review *on* Computing Theatre.

Judith Thompson: I just couldn't work without a computer now. I find I just love working on it. And I always look forward to it. I love the look of it, the way the letters appear. It's like what people say about crack, or cigarettes. I love the feel of it, the sound when it comes on. Don't you? Really, from the moment that the computer arrived, on the table here.

Ric Knowles: How long have you been using a computer?

JT: Just three or four years. I was much later than everybody else. I haven't written a stage play on computer. Radio plays, and lots of scripts, but I haven't written a dramatic play. I did *Hedda Gabler* [an adaptation for the Shaw Festival in 1991] on the typewriter. *Lion in the Streets* was written on a typewriter. I didn't have a computer then. You keyed it in, so you were the first computer connection I had. So the play I write this year will be the first one. You know, it almost wrecked my career—in screenwriting, not in playwriting—because I could never find the $4000, which you just have to find, to buy a computer. So I would hand in these disgraceful manuscripts to *Street Legal*—places like that— and because they wanted me they'd hire a secretary to type them over. But I had come right to the end of my rope. My agent was saying "you have to get one, or you can't go on."

RK: What do you use the computer for?

JT: Just as a word processor, really. A sophisticated typewriter.

RK: Do you compose at it?

JT: Yes. I've written lots of radio plays, and film scripts on computer. And I like it. This last filmscript [*The Wives of Bath*, an adaptation of the Susan Swann novel] is the most successful I've written. The narrative worked with character on the first draft, right away. It just worked out. Every director they've sent it to wants to do it. It really turned out well, and partly why it turned out so well is, instead of writing completely blind, which I often do—I just see it and worry about structure more in the second or third draft—I did this sort of poetic character stuff blind, but I kept working out narrative on pen and paper on the side.

I actually did a sort of "scene one, scene two, that's how this happens," and then I'd do another one the next day, till it worked out like a puzzle. And that helped so much. I'd follow that plan on the computer rather than just guess.

RK: So you're starting with structure now, instead of character?

JT: Yeah, or somehow at the same time. That really works the best.

RK: Do you think its because you're using the computer that you can do that?

JT: Maybe yes, in a sense, because I find when you're writing at the computer you don't get a clear overview unless you print up hard copy and I don't like to do that, except for full drafts. As we were saying earlier, it wastes trees. If you're typewriting you have the pages right there, so you are more likely to read it. I do always start at the beginning on the computer, but still, you're too inside it. So I think printouts can help in that sense.

RK: So you do print off copies and edit them?

JT:Not until the first draft is finished. This is what happens, say, in the case of the Elizabeth Smart filmscript. I knew I wouldn't print it off, so I asked them to make me a copy. And I started going through it and seeing very clearly all the stuff that had to be done, wiping out pages. ... But then when I got to the computer the whole thing changed anyway. I reimagined it. It wasn't enough to just polish the first draft, and tweak it, I had to re-imagine the whole thing, because I'd been too faithfully adapting.

RK: So even printing off hard copy between drafts doesn't help a whole lot.

JT: I think it would help, it helps you to see it clearly. That the whole thing is wrong. You see the thing as a whole, which I don't think I do, reading on the computer. The forest for the trees.

RK: Do you block sections, and move them?

JT: Yes. Scenes, I do. When I look closely at the narrative, and see this should come before that, and so on. It makes it easier.

RK. How exactly do you go about composing and editing?

JT: I start back at the beginning every day, and if I was on a typewriter I wouldn't do that. If I was on a typewriter, I'd go to the last page. I *would* read through the earlier pages, but I'd be less likely to put them back in and rework them. On the computer I go right back to the beginning. And it's annoying sometimes, because with the baby, for example, I'll have two-and-a-half hours to work, and I'll spend two of those hours re-doing the first five pages, totally editing as I go, and so I'll end up only being one page ahead at the end of a two-and-a-half to three-hour day. But then the deadline moves closer and I get less conscientious. So the first 20 pages are crystal perfect, and then ... [*laughs*]. But it's good. I rewrite like I never would have before, on the typewriter. There'll be seventeen drafts of the first twenty pages....

RK: Do you think that the actual physical feel of writing on the computer, as opposed to handwriting or typing, changes or affects your style, or changes your access to …

JT: Yeah, it's much more fluid. It's much easier. Handwriting would be impossible. My hand cramps up writing a *letter* now. The typewriter—all that clank clank clank—interferes a bit. The computer's so fluid. I liked the typewriter, but not as much because of the difficulty of making changes. It's our innate laziness. Because I try to write my first draft without any censorship, I need something that flows fast.

RK: So you find that you're freer to let yourself go because you know how easy it is to change things?

JT: Oh, yes. I mean I used to just cry when I went to a story meeting. It was just sort of adolescent petulance. I didn't want to do the work. I mean "*you* do it!" Especially when it was almost like secretarial work, changing this to this. Now it's no problem. It's fun. I always have fun. Whereas with typewriters, and whiteout … How did we ever survive it?

RK: It's interesting, your excitement. It seems to me that you're somebody that the ease of editing and changing things on the computer would give the freedom of access to the unconscious without having to worry about whether it's right or not the first time around.

JT: That's true. So I can do a big sloppy kind of gushing forth without thinking, "oh, all this is terrible stuff."

RK: So in a sense you're the perfect person for computers. Like you, I don't know much about them—this interview with you will be the low-tech end of this *CTR* issue—and that's the point. They seem, at least, to allow you to forget about the technology and free you to just work.

JT: Yes.

RK: Do you think there's a recognizable difference in the work since you started using a computer? Could somebody from the outside say, "oh, her work changed there."

JT: It's hard to know if it's computers or maturity. I would say the structure is much tighter now, or more integral. It just seems more important to me now.

RK: Do you think that actually shows up in the so-called product?

JT: It'll show up in the film scripts, absolutely.

RK: Does it give you more control, as opposed to some editor saying that you've got to structure it differently?

JT: Oh, yeah. But also I just have a greater sense of structure myself.

RK: What about rehearsals and workshops, and the ability that the computer gives to generate new drafts so quickly?

JT: I know that when I go into rehearsals with this next play, I'll be able to come home at night and work, and it'll be so much easier.

RK: Do you think that's a good thing or a bad thing?

JT: I don't know. You can go too far. What I noticed in the *I Am Yours* workshop is that I was over-responding to the actor. Not to their suggestions so much, but, for instance, Stephen Ouimette is a very comic actor. Everything's funny. And I was loving that so much in the workshop that I made Toi goofier and goofier. And then when Geordie [Johnson] came in for the production, he was every bit as good, but completely different, much more serious, and deadly. Which is ultimately better, I think. So that's dangerous—you get over-excited in rehearsal, and you make changes. I think maybe I'm mature enough now not to do that.

RK: I noticed in *Lion* that you often made changes during or after a rehearsal and then changed back later to the way it was originally.

JT: Did I? Yeah, so the change would be a response to the immediate situation.

RK: Yes. I remember going home and changing things on my computer and then later putting it back close to the way it originally was. Not so much when you cut lines and scenes, but when you made the kinds of changes you're talking about, character changes, often in response to what somebody did, or at somebody's suggestion. A few days later, or a week later, it would end up back, pretty close to the way it was in the first place.

JT: Yeah, I really learned from that, that you have to be very calm and unemotional, and just say, "I'll think about it."

RK: Have you ever tried dictating into a tape recorder?

JT: No, I haven't.

RK: Because the way you write is more or less by getting in character. Even in *Lion*, it was fascinating to see you get into character as an actor would, and write from that space. I can imagine you walking around the room and just speaking the script, composing on your feet.

JT: I may try that. I usually feel that I can do it without having to speak; but I certainly do it to fix up little scenes, where I haven't inhabited properly.

RK: I remember you doing that with *Lion in the Streets*, sending us all out of the room, and walking around the space.

JT: Yes, I had to.

RK: So that's a different feel altogether than sitting at a computer, or typewriter?

JT: Well, you just know then that it's right. I can't make a mistake that way, because my ear is very good, and I'll know if something can't be said or acted. Whereas I don't always know perfectly through my fingers. Something can be unwieldy to say, or too obvious. I mean, I always go for the most obvious, so that I understand the subjects myself, in the first draft. And that's what's wonderful on the computer, I can just go through and say, "no, that's *underneath*—let's have them say the *line*." All the basic things.

RK: What about archives and papers? I think of the fact that we've got all these archives at Guelph, like the handwritten manuscripts of George Walker, or Tomson Highway. There are two things going on there. First, the "archiving" of manuscripts is great for scholars and critics. We've got that complete record, all the drafts, the documented working process; but we may not have that anymore, with changes being done in the computer.

JT: That's a very good point. You'll be able to get first and second drafts and so on, but you won't get all the little drafts and changes in between.

RK: The second thing, which might concern you, is that with manuscripts or typescripts you could get tax write-offs, or even sell your papers, eventually. If you don't any longer have handwritten copies, or versions that have that kind of documentary "authority"—

JT: They won't even exist anymore, will they? I guess there's writing and editing by hand *on* a computer draft, if you do that. I'm going to have to start making hand marks.

RK: Or go back later and make "original" hand-written copies from the printouts.

JT: [*laughs*] Yeah. It would be worth it.

RK: I was careful with *Lion in the Streets* to date and save pages, daily, so there would be a record.

JT: Really!

RK: Yes. I've got a cardboard box full of papers from that workshop. Do you do that sort of thing?

JT: No.

RK: So the revision process just gets "disappeared"?

JT: It gets disappeared. And that is too bad. I do so much revising. Because, say I'm going through the first eight pages of this Elizabeth Smart thing, I'll revise the dialogue at least once every day, for three weeks. You feel that every word has to be perfect, like a piece of music. But you don't save all those changes.

RK: So it's not possible to track people's revision process like you used to be able to do. And there's also the problem that there isn't that documentary "authority" in a printout, which after all is infinitely reproducible. If it's handwritten, you know who wrote it, and you can see the changes they've made.

JT: And anyone can get hold of a disk. In film, producers certainly do, and make changes. I wonder why the writer is so much less valued in film than in theatre? In film, on pretty well all contracts, the director gets a polish, an "independent polish." It infuriates me.

RK: Do they usually take full advantage of that clause, without consulting you?

JT: Well, they haven't all done that, but it's what I'm worried about with *Wives of Bath*, and *Elizabeth*. And that's what I had the big falling out with Patricia Rozema over. I just said, "would you mind, when you do the polish, let's just consult so that I can do the changes, so we maintain just one voice?" She said "you are not having the final cut on my film." So I'd like to get together with a lot of writers and do something about that. What the agents all say is, "it's the producer's product, because they initiated it."

RK: Good old capitalism.

JT: So we just have to say "no" to them. "Find another writer." If we get all the best writers, that everybody wants, to agree to say no.

RK: Anything else?

JT: Yes. I think with computers you can keep your office more tidy.

(1994)

No Soy Culpable

by Judith Thompson

"I AM INOCENT."

That's one of the first things we saw after stepping off the plane in Mexico City: a Wanted poster on the wall, with three walleyed, wide-faced men, and someone had written "I am inocent," with one n, in pen across the poster. As we walked into the Mexican air, we were approached by several Mexican men bellowing at us in broken English to come with them. But our tourist guide-booklets advised us to hire only official taxis, so that's what we did.

In the back of the rickety old taxi, which bumped and sped along the road to Mexico City, I felt stunned and slightly dreadful, the way I used to feel as a child with a new babysitter, or at a strange cousin's house. There was just that tiny chance that things would never be the same. I have not travelled much at all in the past twenty years because, I am embarrassed to say, I have been afraid to. I have used valid excuses: no money and no time, and one, two, and then three children, but the truth is that I inwardly resist any travel at all, even to Kingston, three hours away from Toronto. I have turned down trips to Russia and Sweden and England, because of this fear.

Of what?

Not flying, not danger, and certainly not the unfamiliar.

I am hungry for the unfamiliar. And I got lots of it in Mexico City. I was awestruck right away by the sight of the coloured tin and cardboard shacks on either side of the road. They were piled and crammed into an above-ground under-ground city. There were hanging plants and bright and white clothing dancing from lines. And although I guessed that these were the homes of the poorest Mexican people, and represented all that was atrocious in the Mexican system, they were beautiful, because people had made them to live in. Just after that, my breath was taken away by a fifteen-foot Marlboro Man on top of a building, astride a bucking, twenty-foot horse. With a cigarette hanging out of his mouth. I remembered that the actual Marlboro man is dead, of lung cancer. Canada and Mexico have America between them, and all over them.

The streets of this city of ten million were almost deserted. And although there was a scattering of intriguing, unfamiliar, twisted trees, there were almost no flowers. The air had poisoned them. It was early July, and I had come ready for heat with six sun-dresses. And one light sweater. And sandals, with no socks at all. I hadn't consulted even the weather channel. I was going to be slightly chilled the whole time. And damp. It rains every day in Mexico City in July, from around four in the afternoon on.

I was with a group of Canadian artists and arts administrators invited by the Mexican government and sent by External Affairs; we were lodged in luxury at the Stouffer Presidente, a big concrete warehouse for rich persons, which offered us rooms at less than half price. The hotel is located in Polanco, a wealthy area with embassies and Benettons and internationally renowned museums and astonishing Spanish-style mansions with twenty-foot wrought-iron fences and turrets and tiled courtyards, and, of course, round-the-clock security guards. The Stouffer Presidente itself had at least thirty policemen armed with semi-automatics patrolling the hotel twenty-four hours a day. This made me feel safe and threatened at the same time.

UNICEF was hosting a Conference of Mayors at the Stouffer Presidente. Mayors from around the world had been invited by UNICEF to attend a conference on child poverty. Every morning we would see them gathered, waiting for their bus in their wildly varied national dress, talking joyfully to one another. It gave me a glimmer of hope, until I learned that the Stouffer Presidente is owned by the Nestlé corporation, the same corporation that has been practically forcing baby formula on Third World mothers, deceiving them into thinking that mother's milk is in some way inferior. Odd. Like holding a conference on the well-being of mice in a boa-constrictor.

In the hotel there was a tour business, of course, and because my companion was writing about Hemingway, I agreed to go to a bullfight. I have always abhorred the idea of bullfights, but I told myself it was time to see what it was that I abhorred. After all, I couldn't stop it by not going, and by going I would have a deeper understanding, maybe, of the whole thing. So, we bought our tickets for fifty dollars American each, I still can't believe we paid that, and we were picked up by a shiny dark-red minivan. My companion and me, a Filipino mayor and his wife, a bullfight nut from Illinois and his wife, two rather gruff young Korean men, and a couple of others I don't remember. It took us about twenty-five minutes to get to the stadium. Okay, I thought to myself, in Canada that would have cost us eight to ten dollars. We were taken into the stadium for free, while others paid two pesos. Okay, we were at ten to twelve dollars. Canadian. The stadium was almost empty. This was because it was the winter season, and we would see only the novice toreadors. The stadium was all eroding cold stone, and we bought cushions to sit on. We sat for a very long time while our guide told us about McDonald's and other large corporations spreading around rumours that the tortillas made and sold by street vendors caused cholera. Suddenly there was a fanfare, and the young toreadors came on. They were stylish, in colourful, skin-tight pants and bolero jackets and theatrical capes, and they did what looked like a minimalist modern dance, full of pose and attitude. It was quite striking. Then the bull was released.

It stood in the centre, still for a moment, and looked around. I thought its heart was beating fast. One of them poked it. It moved. Another poked it again. It ran. It was poked again, and it ran faster, around the edge of the circle. Every time it slowed down it was poked again. Occasionally it fake-lunged at one of its tormentors, but mostly it just ran in circles. Finally one of the toreadors took up his big decorated party stick and plunged it into the bull. I gasped. Our guide, sensing my dismay, explained to me that it was important to bleed the bull, because otherwise it would suffer a heart attack. Because of the fear. I looked back at the bull, standing quite still as the swordstick thing dangled from its side, and thick blood dripped from the wound. The bull was at this point still strong, and running hard, with dark, terrified eyes, and all I could think of was a young woman in Ontario who was kidnapped and murdered. I thought, God have mercy, is this what it was like? At the beginning, when she was pulled into the car, and she was still strong, and fighting, and not sure what was going on, and had some hope? Neither she nor the bull could have known that their death was a certainty. We knew that the bull would die, because we had been told that we would see five bulls die. The bulls always die. My breakfast came up into my mouth and I asked the guide to drive me back to the hotel, considering the exorbitant amount of money I had paid to his company. He refused, so I told my companion I was leaving, and I left. The tourist guide-book said that it is deeply insulting to leave the stadium; it said the savage wild beast in the ring bears no relation to its barnyard cousin in North America. But it looked exactly like the bulls I see at my cousin's dairy farm outside of London, Ontario. Sitting in the taxi, I reflected that the slaughterhouses of North America are no kinder than the bullrings of Mexico, and yet I participate in the slaughter. I hold a leather shoulder bag. Many of my shoes have been leather. At least at the bullfight the public confronts its participation in the slaughter of animals.

In the next few days, whenever I had time away from the conference, we filled ourselves with the unfamiliar. Here are some moments that have stayed with me:

Young clowns wearing orange wigs and big red feet and tear-drop big-mouth make-up, just standing on streetcorners. They didn't juggle, or blow up balloons, or sing silly songs. They just stood. When I smiled at one of them, he stared at me as if to say, "What are you smiling at you stupid bitch," and looked away.

There were mothers sleeping in the small parks with their children all wrapped up in the same shawl/blanket. It looked to me as if they had walked for twenty to thirty miles to come and sell their dolls and scarves to the tourists. But there weren't any tourists, there was only us.

A little boy of about four watched me as I looked at old photographs of the Mexican revolution. I smiled at him, and he very quietly asked me, I guessed, for money. I gave him a few pesos, which he quickly pocketed, and then he disappeared.

There were dogs everywhere. Old and dusty, lopey Mexican dogs, just wandering, mostly on their own, about the city. Often they would lie in the middle of the sidewalk, and people would step over them. We stepped up to a very expensive restaurant, which was closed, to admire the shrubbery, when I noticed an ear perk up. I looked more closely and saw three dogs sleeping, completely hidden by the small bushes.

From the windows of our velvety, noiseless bus, we saw a tiny girl, about two years old, tottering on the edge of the curb in a crinoline dress, screaming. Cars were speeding by. We looked for the mother and finally saw her, at the far end of this "island," holding up her homemade dolls in the hope that passing cars would stop, and buy. She had no expression in her face at all, and in the whole five minutes we watched, she did not look at her child once. The child would learn, we decided, in a matter of months, not ever to cry.

The Zocolo, or main square, bordered by the National Palace and the Cathedral and other magnificent old seventeenth-century (I think) buildings. The Zocolo was occupied. Farmers from the country were living in large tents, in the middle of the square, and protesting Free Trade, among other things. The farmers were very striking, dressed in the same style of clothing that their fathers and grandfathers and great-grandfathers had probably worn. When we came out of the National Palace after seeing the unforgettable historical murals of Diego Rivera— depicting, among other things, the torture of the Incas by the conquering Spaniards—hundreds of farmers, male and female, stood facing us silently, holding up a banner with large, black letters. Their silence was penetrating.

Trapped in a labyrinthine market wide enough only for one and a half of us, full of shoes and bowls and jeans and sponges; thousands of stalls, sheets and curtains dividing them. Freshly made tortillas with curried chicken and meat and onion and bright green sauces, and pale green fruit in plastic bags, and apples cut into pieces and covered in paprika, mango or melon carved into the shape of a rose and sold on a stick; pineapple, freshly squeezed juices, and Chiclets and Diet Coke, and tamarind nectar.

Back from the conference at four o'clock one day, we caught a taxi to the pyramids, about twenty miles out of the city. The taxi driver was a nice older man who had been to Chicago in the seventies at the invitation of an appreciative tourist, but he hadn't liked it because all the houses, he said, were the same colour. He wondered how people could live in a place where buildings were the same colour. Mexicans paint their adobe houses bright blues and pinks and oranges.

Once at the pyramids, we were tackled by a dozen or so vendors of hideous, mass-produced trinkets: "I made it myself in my home." We had just learned that the pyramids closed at five and it was already ten to, so we ran, hoping to climb to the top. It seemed very important to climb to the top. We had been told that these were ancient Mayan pyramids, built to honour the sun god and the moon god. I had read about the human sacrifices; young girls who were carried up to the top of the pyramid, calm and content in the knowledge that they were dying for their people. I wondered if they had any fear at all, of the knife above their heads, I wondered if they fainted and cried when the knife plunged into their chests, and the priest carved out their hearts as an offering to the sun god. Did their mothers have even a moment of doubt? Suddenly, a dozen guards blew their whistles and shouted at us in Spanish. They were ordering us off the pyramids. The sheepish taxi driver, who of course hadn't told us about the five o'clock closing, whisked us away to a nearby shop which sold silver. He clearly had some arrangement with the owners. We reluctantly accepted their offer of free tequila and lemon, knowing that we couldn't afford to buy anything. We looked around, and ooohed and aaahed, and then said we'd like to go back. They did not smile when they said goodbye.

The night before we left, we saw a Mexican play, which was not on our itinerary. It was about a family that lived in the tin and cardboard shacks by the airport. Although we could not understand the words, the play was clear. There is nothing beautiful about the lives of these people who must live in boxes, with no water and no heat and no toilet. They are full of despair, and hatred for themselves and others. Many of the young people sniff a substance which makes them blind and demented. The mother must put her son on a leash and throw a can around his neck in the hope that kind strangers will deposit coins. She drags her son and her most precious possession, a tortilla cooker, along with her to the street. But if McDonald's and the other big U.S. corporations have their way, nobody will buy her tortillas anymore. At the end of this powerful play, the cast stood silently behind a banner which read something like "The Terrible Silence." The tiny audience clapped, and we all left full of shame.

On our last night we were taken to a bar/nightclub on the second floor of an old rundown house in a fairly busy area. It was called Paquita's, after the woman who owned the place and sang for her patrons on the weekends. The place was a disappointment at first, mainly because the snack food had been altered for our palates. Instead of the real Mexican food we had all begun to love, we were served slabs of bland generic cheese and canned ham, and supermarket tacos with no hotsauce. "*Salsa piquante, por favor,*" we cried, and finally got it. The first two singers were passable, and we continued our lively sangria-drenched conversations over the music. But the third, this was Paquita. In our sickening middle-class way, we began to snicker quietly—she wore a harsh, sunset-coloured, skin-tight lamé dress to the ground, slit up to the crotch, and silver lamé platform shoes, more make-up than a drag queen on St. Laurent, and she was a good size 22. But the moment she started to sing all snickering stopped. The suffering, the intelligence, the life of the woman filled her voice and her face; her eyes looked through us behind our faces and found us.

When we were changing planes in Houston, Texas, the Customs man said he had a brother up in Canada, in Ottawa. He said his brother told him that Canada was going to hell because of open immigration, that all these so-called refugees were draining the blood of the country and making men like his brother poor. Our smiles froze, and we answered him with our silence. I was frightened of this man. I knew that if I had answered him with the torrent of words gathering at the back of my teeth, he could have stopped us, and searched our luggage, and perhaps planted drugs or pistols in our bags. So we said nothing, and he waved us on through. In the plane to Toronto, I squirmed with guilt about my silence, and its inadequacy. Its Canadian-ness. Then I remembered the farmers in the Zocolo, gathered, facing us, using their silence.

I bought a tape of Paquita, and when I play it for friends they laugh, and say they've heard her in gay bars, or isn't she great, but they don't get it. I guess they'd have to see her eyes.

What was I afraid of? I think, judging from my feeling of relief as we landed at Pearson, I was afraid that I would not be able to get back. I was afraid that all technology would fail, and I would be stranded, a stranger in an unfamiliar place, with no voice to speak with, no words to be understood. Now I peruse the travel section of the paper and I fantasize about far-off places. I know, almost, that Canada does not disappear when I leave it. And I know that I do not disappear when I leave Canada.

(1994)

Look to the Lady: Re-examining Women's Theatre

by Judith Thompson, edited by Soraya Peerbaye

Excerpt from "Art in Your Face," a panel held in March 1995 during Nightwood Theatre's tenth annual Groundswell Festival.

> *Clean jeans, and comfortable shoes*
> *I need no secrets here at home*
> *in this echoless light.*
> *I spread my papers out around me.*
> *Opposite, alert, a grey-eyed lady takes fire,*
> *one pale nostril quivering.*
> *We both know women who take up space*
> *are called sloppy.*
>   Audre Lorde, "Syracuse Airport" (22)

Making theatre is taking up space, and so I thought this poem felt appropriate, both to me as a person because I've always been accused of being sloppy, and as a theatre artist. I guess I've always felt that it's not a very lady-like thing to do … I started being unladylike at a very early age. My penmanship was always marked "sloppy" on every report card from Junior Kindergarten on … And I've only recently realized that in a way, it was my first act of sabotage … And that was my first act of theatre …

Theatre has to be embarrassing, and theatre has to be slovenly … When I have young babies I like to let my breast milk leak through my blouse in public at nice restaurants. I will not wear those breast pads! And the looks of disgust on people's faces are the same looks on the people that walk out of my plays. I've let something leak that's not supposed to be leaking …

Growing up a girl, and a Catholic girl at that, means I grew up bound. I grew up with a psyche bound like the feet of women in ancient China, mangled and bloody, but that's what the men like. That arouses them. And a mask had been created for me … a ridiculous theatrical fey mask of a girl, and I stepped into it as soon as I could talk and inhabited it thoroughly … And then, a little later, desperate for some qualities to make me a little more than just a paper doll in a huge chain, I created the character of Judith. I created a sort of absent-minded, chronically late, unco-ordinated character … This would make people laugh … It would make them remember me, even if in scorn. And it was my second act of sabotage.

But there was a resistance fighter inside me, a stranger that I didn't know, somehow still alive. This stranger asserted herself first in this lack of physical co-ordination, because it illustrated the schism between my private and public self, and then in Grand Mal seizures ... My face turned dark purple in one and I almost died. I think, I'm sure now, that I almost died basically of being a girl.

The next seizure was *The Crackwalker*. And with each play the resistance became stronger ... Joan of Arc was sentenced to life in prison in 1431 for leading the uprising against the English, but she was burned to death for resuming her habit in prison of dressing as a male. The judge said, time and time again, you have relapsed as a dog that returns to its vomit ... Each time we write or make theatre, we are being disobedient. We are donning male clothes like Joan of Arc, in the sense that we have the magic power that has been held by males ...

When I was starting out, [there were] these wonderful older men who ... really wanted to *help* me ... And then when I wouldn't do what I was told they became extremely hostile. My first experience with *The Crackwalker* at Passe Muraille was a girl nightmare ... I was the *idiot savant* who'd somehow vomited out a chaotic mess, and [the director] was going to fix it and make it into a play ...

I think men are insanely jealous of female creativity, starting of course with our ability to create life. We cannot underestimate their hatred. So we need safe places, I think, where we don't have to fight the tedious, exhausting fight ... Creating is dangerous, it costs all of us a great deal. So we need to go somewhere where we can really spread out our papers like Audre Lorde says, and take up space, and not appease anybody.

(1995)

Work Cited

Lorde, Audre. "Syracuse Airport." *The Marvelous Arithmetics of Distance (Poems 1987-1992)*. New York: Norton, 1993.

Mouthful of Pearls

by Judith Thompson

A young woman named Sonja was walking alone at night in one of Toronto's ravines, when a man emerged from the bushes. Sonja glanced at him and, not wanting to show him fear, continued walking at the same pace. He followed, and soon caught up with her, walking alongside her. He then moved in front of her and blocked her way.

Sonja: Excuse me.

Man: Yes?

Sonja: Would you let me pass?

Man: Sure, sure, no problem. I … just I saw you and I was just wanting to know if you knew about that … part.

Sonja: Part?

Man: Down in the ravine. The more secret part, right? You know that part? It's very nice. I think you'd like it.

Sonja: Please, don't touch me.

Man: I just thought I could take you there.

Sonja: No, thank you, I'm enjoying my walk.

Man: It's not too far out of your way. Come on.

Sonja: Please don't touch me.

Man: I'm not gonna eat you. What's the matter?

Sonja: I would just like to continue my walk, if you don't mind.

Man: Well, why not walk with me? I'm the best walker around. I could show ya parts of the ravine I bet you never seen. Marsh grasses growin' twenty foot high, and wildflowers with colours you don't see anywheres else, magenta, burnt yellows and oranges splittin' and splittin' their gooey white juice.

Sonja: Thank you, but I would like to walk alone. Take your hand off me, please.

Man: Alone? What are ya, nuts? There's real bad guys out there, you know, just waitin' for a loveliesque woman like you. So softy-nice.

Sonja: I don't feel I need protection, and I like my own company. Please let me pass.

Man: Wait a minute, just wait a minute. You don't like me 'cause you think I'm down and out, but you got it all wrong. Oh yeah. Listen. I could give you more than you ever dreamed of. I gotta deal I'm workin' on, a big big deal, I been workin' on it for two years now, it's a muffin business, ya see muffins are the thing, all the businesses, the hospitals, the cafeterias all around the city they're after the big muffin, the perfect light, tasty, the healthy, the low fat the oatmeal and apricot and the money is going to rain on me, babe, just rain on down. So stick with me, babe, you'll have a mouthful of pearls.

Sonja: Let go of me, and listen, listen to me. I'm not interested. I'm not interested in any of that. I had it. I was vice-president at the TD Bank, pulling in 500,000 a year; I had a house in Forest Hill, a farm in Caledon with a guest house, an ex-husband, a summer house in Chester, Nova Scotia, two children, a nanny, a full-time housekeeper, I read the R.O.B. and nothing else, everything, everything was acquisition. One day, about five years ago, it was around seven thirty, I got home from work, I was in the kitchen, chatting with the nanny, playing with my kids, and my four-year-old, Julia, she'd been balancing on the kitchen chair, and it fell backwards. She hit her head on the dog's food bowl and she was screaming and crying and I ran to her and she pushed me away. She cried, "I want Felice," that's her nanny, and she wouldn't let me touch her. And then, that night, my son Michael was having a bad dream, about draculas and he cried for Felice. I went in and sat on his bed and he slapped my face and he cried inconsolably. The next day I quit my job. I had to sell the house and now we live all together in one large room. The kids love it. They say it's cozy, like living in a nice hotel room. We all watch TV in bed together and read stories and snuggle and have a great time. My sister's with them now. She comes so I can walk and think and know who I am. Do you know who you are?

Man: You have kids?

Sonja: DO YOU KNOW WHO YOU ARE?

Man: I'm a lover.

Sonja: Where is your soul? When do you feel it?

Man: When I seen you. Your beauty made it rise up.

Sonja: That is not about your soul.

Man: Come here.

Sonja: No, I will not come there. I'm going to continue my walk. Good night.

Man: I said come here.

He grabs her.

Sonja: What is it you want from me, exactly?

Man: You know what I want.

Sonja: No. I don't.

Man: I will toll upon your belly.

Sonja: What?

Man: I will toll, like a bell, upon your silver white belly.

Sonja: Let go of me.

Man: Will you marry me?

Sonja: Let go of me now.

Man: I want to dress you in lace and bone china and kiss your pretty green eyes over and over.

Sonja: My eyes aren't green.

Man: Crazy eyes.

Sonja: You want my eyes.

Man: Lookin' at me. Lookin' at my body. I been workin' out, you know. Got a stomach like a rock.

Sonja: Why do you want me to look at you? Why?

Man: Because. You're beautiful. You musta been told that before.

Sonja: Beautiful. What do you mean by beautiful?

Man: Like a magazine cover, you know, so nice and slim, not like that bag my ex-wife, all that long blonde hair, and those long dancer's legs ya got, perfect, and and the joyful bosom there, and and…

Sonja: My body will sag and die like everyone else's. I'll get fat when I'm forty, it runs in my family, my joyful bosom will probably fill with cancer, varicose veins will cover my legs and my knees and hips will have to be replaced. And I'll get cataracts over these crazy eyes. Then will I be beautiful?

Man: Come on, let's go into the bush. Now.

Sonja: What do you want from me?

Man: I want to devour you.

> *He laughs, and kisses her, growling like a dog. She struggles to get away. She is breathless when she speaks.*

Sonja: Listen to me. Please, just listen to me and then kill me if you must. Just ask yourself what it is you really want from me. Really. What do you want?

Man: When you're on fire, you jump in the water, babe. You don't stop to ask questions.

Sonja: I am talking to you. Talk to me, I'm a person.

> *He takes a long knife from his pocket. She gasps.*

Sonja: What's that?

Man: Just my hunting knife.

Sonja: Let me go.

Man: You come into this ravine lookin' for me. You been lookin' for me all your life.

Sonja: I came looking for wilderness.

Man: And what did you find?

Sonja: A predator. Stay away from me.

Man: I want you.

Sonja: No, you don't.

Man: I'm going to have you.

Sonja: You'll never have me. You can tear my body apart with your knife but you'll never reach me.

Man: Your eyes drives me wild, I think about your eyes and I toll like the bell.

Sonja: You want my eyes?

Man: I want your eyes to stroke me, stroke me with your eyes, come on, baby.

Sonja: You want my eyes?

Man: Oooh look at your face, fightin' face, blood red with anger, how come you're so mad, eh pretty? How come you're so mad?

Sonja: Because I'm tired of it, I hate it, I HATE IT! Ever since I was ten years old the men have been staring at me, wanting to devour me, all because I have blonde hair and a big bust. I couldn't walk down the street. Even down the aisle at church. In school, boys would whisper when I passed, and when they talked to me it was the way a wolf might talk to a rabbit, always with the devouring on their minds, always, always. I hate your desire.

Man: You liar. All you girls, you love gettin' looked at. Even my four-year-old, you should see her, preening in the mirror.

Sonja: I hate you. I HATE you.

Man: I love it when those sexy eyes of yours flash. I'd love those eyes to flash on my secret parts.

She takes the knife.

Man: Whatcha doin' with that knife? Give it back to me right now. OOOOh I like a wild girl. Come on, honey, give it here.

She cuts out her left eye.

Man: Holy Christ in heaven. Whatcha doin', man? You crazy witch. Hey! Hellllp!

Sonja: You want my eye? Here is my eye. Take it! Take it!

Man: Ahhhh. Stop that, come on. Stop it. Christ. This … this … isn't what I meant. (*He shouts out*) Hellllp.

Sonja: Yes it is. It is what you meant.

Man: You're a freak. Look at ya, blood drippin' all over you. You're crazy.

Sonja: And now I will cut off my hand, and then it will touch you anytime you want. Anywhere you want. All your secret parts.

Man: No! Please!

Sonja: There. Now you have my eye to look at you and my hand to touch you. Would you like my lips? To kiss you, to whisper in your ear?

Man: You keep away from me, freak. Get these things offa me, why are they stickin' to me? Get them offa me.

> *The man runs away, screaming, with her eye and hand and lip sticking to him. The woman kneels down.*

Sonja: Oh, my good God in heaven, forgive me. Why did I give in to my rage, why did I do this? How will I watch over my children in the playground with only one eye, or see all their sweet heads on their pillows, how will I feed them and dress them with one hand, and how will I sing to them or whisper my love with no mouth? Oh! God forgive me.

And she lay down on the wet grass and fell unconscious from loss of blood. A group of teenagers who were heading down for a drinking party spotted her, and horrified by her disfigurement, covered her with their coats and sent the fastest runner in their group to call for help. The ambulance attendants found her hand and her eye and her lip strewn along the path and brought them to the hospital where the surgeons sewed them back on.

The man told the story of the "crazy" woman he met in the ravine at different Toronto bars every night. It was the only time in his life people had been fascinated by him, and looked at him while he talked. He felt a warm flush through his body; he felt like a star. After he told his story, the listeners would shake their heads and ask him why a woman would do something like that.

"I really don't know," he would say, very quietly. And everybody looked at the floor. And before he left the bar, he always lowered his voice and said: "And this was a really pretty woman, right? Like, she was your fantasy girl."

But when he walked up Yonge Street he no longer stared at the young, heavily made-up girls leaning against the storefronts; for every time he looked, even by accident, at a girl, his eyeball would burn, and his hand would become infected and painful, and his mouth would fill with canker sores. Unfortunately, fear and pain were the only things that stopped him looking, for he still did not see anything wrong with the way he looked at the girls.

The woman lived with physical pain and discomfort for the rest of her life, but she lived in peace, because no man ever looked at her again with devouring eyes.

(1995)

Second Thoughts (What I'd Be If I Were Not a Writer)
by Judith Thompson

If I were not a writer I think I would wear a riding hat. With a steel lining. Because I would be having many more epileptic seizures than I do presently. Because any of the non-writer-real jobs I have had caused me sleepless nights, self disgust, swollen eyes, cystic acne, and eating disorders, all of which increased electrical activity in my brain, which, I believe, increases the frequency of seizures. For instance, while I was employed typing passports for Canada House, in London, England. I would often feel a seizure coining on while travelling on the two-tiered London bus, and be compelled to lie down. Once I felt so dizzy I lay down across the entrance to a London subway, being from a small town and unfamiliar with subway etiquette. Many people stepped over me, a few asked after me. The combination of the extreme boredom of typing passports, the smell of the "white-out," which I had to use constantly, and the intense fluorescent lighting in the passport office made it almost impossible to stay awake; I often fell asleep on the keyboard and jerked awake drooling shortly afterwards. And it would still only be ten forty-five.

I would not be a passport typist if I were not a writer.

My very first job was as a nurse's aide in a home for chronic-care geriatrics. I was eighteen. I had never had a job. I had never even really cleaned my room, or set the table properly. But, as I told the hospital job person, I "really love old people." Judging from the behaviour of most of the nurse's aides I worked with, this was not an issue. When the nurses and doctors weren't looking, the elderly patients were, for the most part, handled roughly and spoken to with hostility and disdain. I saw fist-sized bedsores filled with maggots, and emptied urine bags and cleaned the bodies of dead patients with PhisoHex. My hair and skin always smelled of PhisoHex and Death, and no amount of washing would remove it. After a few months, the hospital stopped calling me in, because though I was loving and kind with the patients, I was fairly incompetent as far as the practical side of the job went. I was relieved, because the other aides, after finding out that I was involved in the theatre, despised me, and it was unpleasant to work with all that resentment as well as all that dying. Once, as a sort of test, a few of them dragged me into the TV room to look at a soap opera and asked me, sniggering, "Is this good?"

If I were not a writer I would not be a nurse's aide. Or a passport typist.

My first waitressing job was at Dainty Dora's at Ontario Place in the summer of 1973. I poured a pitcher of beer over the lap of a customer who suddenly saw the devil in my eyes and he pointed his finger and said, "You did that on purpose." "You called my friend a name," I said, and flounced away. A very old Hungarian man used to come in every Sunday and give me five-dollar tips on every glass of beer and once he even gave me a ring, but one Sunday I forgot to order food for him, and Mike, the fat-necked loud-mouthed pig of a manager, bellowed at me, "Where's his food?" and I arrogantly answered, "He doesn't have any," and he pointed his finger at me and yelled at me to "Pack up." In Ontario in those days you had to order food with a drink on Sundays. I had forgotten about this. I sobbed and howled as loudly as I could while I was "packing up" so as to disturb the customers greatly. Upstairs, as I changed out of my mini-skirted red gingham uniform, I heard him saying "Get her out of here. GET HER OUT OF HERE."

I would not be a waitress if I were not a writer. Or a passport typist. Or a nurse's aide.

I was even fired from working in a grocery store. The owner's wife said to me, "You a lazy girl, such a lazy girl, you only like the sex, and the boys, thinkin' about the boys and the sexy all day long, you lazy, lazy girl." I gave her the most imperious look I could muster and told her I was not thinking of boys or sex, but things much loftier, that I couldn't possibly explain. Like how to make it to five o'clock without passing out from boredom.

Or a grocery store worker.

I haven't experienced boredom once since I became a writer. Not ever. Yet what I remember the most about the non-writer jobs I had is a killing kind of boredom. A feeling of suffocating, of a choke-chain around my neck, a need to put my fist through the window and run run run and never stop. I thank God every day that I am lucky enough to be doing something that I love, because it really is the only thing I can do well. One of my greatest fears, of course, is that I will one day wake up and find myself unable to write. Like a fairy tale, I will have brought this loss upon myself with some act of negligence. I will try associated work such as journalism and fail, because of my lack of organization, and my inability to punctuate and paragraph. I will look through the classified section every day, and circle non-stressful looking jobs, such as plant watering. I will take the plant-watering job, because it is a job for people who've been fired from every other job for being "dreamers." The dreamer needs only a large watering can, and a sense of direction. I would walk from building to building in downtown Toronto, and I would take the stairs more often than the elevator, because it would give me a sense of achievement. I would smile at the receptionist, and perhaps help myself to some coffee with double whitener before watering all the office plants. I would pull off all the brown and wilted leaves. I would care about all of my plants, and know each of them. I don't think I would need the riding hat for this job, because

I would be content. Sometimes I would wake up early and stand at my small third-storey window and see my city, in whitish dawn, with all my plants, waiting for me, growing, and very very still. And I would feel calm.

(1995)

Epilepsy & the Snake: Fear in the Creative Process [1]
by Judith Thompson

Today I am going to talk for a while about pure fear and the loss of the self in the act of creation. Where are the eleven other Judiths?

About ten years ago I woke up early one spring morning in a state of pure fear. For at least a minute, which seemed like forever, I was in a panic, trembling from head to toe, as I couldn't remember where the eleven other Judiths might be. Without them, I had no self. I was disappearing. Although psychologically I can attribute this moment of terror to a change in medications, it gave me some insight into the psychological cost of the work that I do: the creation of other characters within a world that resembles our own, but, like Alice's Wonderland, is seen through the looking glass, darkly.

I have known real fear only a few times in my relatively sheltered life. But I believe those moments of fear are directly connected to the source of creativity within me.

All of my life I have been plagued by frequent dreams of snakes, in which I am reduced to this state of pure fear. My heart is pounding, I feel as if I am shattering, and I always wake up screaming. Naturally, I have asked myself many times what this snake means. I asked a professor of philosophy who was teaching a course I was auditing at the University of Toronto on the history of psychoanalysis. A Freudian, he responded that it meant that I wanted to sleep with my father— because Freudians believe that the dream is the disguised fulfillment of the unconscious wish. His response, of course, was beneath contempt. I am certain beyond any doubt that the snake does not mean that. The snake is something far more fearsome: death, the devil, or, very possibly, a secret that I may never know. And I believe that the only way for me to stop these dreams that plague me is to know the secret. But if I know the secret I may forfeit my gift as a playwright. So I am trapped.

To give you an example:

The other night I dreamt that I had climbed a large sandy mountain in the heat, with a huge snake dangling over my shoulder. Now my fear of snakes is such that I would almost rather have a bullet through my head than a snake over my shoulder. So I was shaking, heart pounding, head reeling. In the dream my companion said, "Look at this, you've travelled all this way with the snake and you are all right.'" And I said, "yes, you're right," and the snake dropped to the ground in a coil, apparently dead, bluish. I looked at it, and was finally able to breathe, seeing it on the ground. As I took a deep breath, the snake leapt up with electric speed and force, and bit and bit and bit, and I screamed and screamed and woke up. Upon waking I was very disappointed, because I had thought that I had finally killed the snake by putting it in *Sled*, the play I am currently working on. I had had a previous dream that someone very close to me was walking towards me, singing softly, with a rattlesnake in a bucket. I implored this person to please not come any closer, and she smiled gently, and murmured, and kept coming closer. I began to scream and scream and jumped awake. Well, I gave this dream to one of my characters, and it solved the mystery of that character. I suddenly understood the play. But still not the snake. And the fear is still immense—even at this moment, every time I type the word, I tremble. As I speak it, I feel slightly nauseous. But I believe that the snake holds the secret in its mouth. And so I will continue to look at it. But fear greatly uncovering it.

The other moments of fear involved seizures. Epileptic seizures. I had my first grand mal epileptic seizure when I was nine years old. I was in church on Sunday morning, it was very warm, and the night before I had watched a popular science fiction show called "The Outer Limits." There had been vampires in it, in a very contemporary, suburban, sixties setting. And I had been very spooked by it; I could smell the blood as I sat on our living room floor and watched the show. The next morning was sunny, the smell of blooming early-summer flowers, blue spruce, and freshly mowed lawns masking the smell of blood. While I was sitting in church, in my pew, I started to feel peculiar. I could smell the blood again. The church was packed, and every sound, every rustle of paper was magnified in my eardrums. I began to sense the presence of vampires. Congregating. Below me, in the party room, where we often had juice and cookies after mass. Their eyes were dark and limpid, their faces stiff and pale, their lips thin, red, and their hair dark, and they all wore velvet capes and pointy, tight shoes, and they were crowded together, beneath my feet, floating together to the ceiling of the party room with all the refreshments waiting in the corner, and like bats they clung by their mouths to the ceiling. Their mouths were directly under my feet. I could feel my body draining of blood as they sucked, pulling the blood from my body to my feet and through my feet into the floor of the church, through the floorboards and sub-floor and soaking the ceiling of the party room, sucking the blood into their mouths, filling up on my nine-year-old blood, so many of them. Oh, I couldn't shake the vision, I knew it couldn't be true. It was time for communion. And I stiffened. And fell like a seventy-pound piece of wood. To the floor.

The seizure is a form of death. One has no choice but to surrender to the darkness and the chaos, and hope one will come out alive on the other end. But there is no guarantee of that. The electrical impulses in the brain are storming, in a state of chaos. The inhibitors, those chemicals that keep things orderly and relatively calm, are not working. When all is restored it is a kind of miracle. I had two or three more seizures, and then was free of them for a couple of years until they took me off the medication again. I was fifteen. I was having a terrible time at school; for that year, I was the one they threw rocks at and made animal noises at, called lewd and vicious names. I sat on the steps with one of my few friends. I had an empty stomach and I felt odd. Suddenly I knew without a doubt that I would have a seizure. Oh no, I said, oh no. It was what it must feel like to have a gun to your head or a knife at your throat, to know that there is no stopping it, none, and the ground opened up with a sickening sound and I fell, head first, down down down into the ground, the yellowish brown, the dark, the voices of the dead, screaming, taking, whispering around me, swirling. I was prodded and poked and stung and pinched as I fell, faster and faster and faster like a dead rocketship falling through space down down, and finally I seemed to have landed, somewhere in the middle of the earth and I absolutely knew that if I didn't scream at that moment, if I didn't scream myself back up, there I would stay forever, dead. I felt that I could see up the dark tunnel hole I had fallen into. I could see life, light, human faces at the tiny opening way, way above me, '"I must scream," I didn't know how, "I must scream up, take a breath, take a breath, scream yourself up," and I did.

The Vice Principal of the school was staring at me, kneeling over me, his big red fleshy face several inches from mine. "What the Heck is all the screaming about?" he asked, as if I had been playing a prank. Apparently my face was dark purple. Which means, of course, I hadn't been breathing. I am sure that I almost died. And there was no white light. No kindly figures. Just horror. And chaos. Perhaps the white light would have been next. I can only hope.

For many years I lived in fear of another seizure. Luckily, I only had a few more, and I am not so fearful any more. But I have learned a great deal from these encounters with death.

I have learned why we fear disorder and chaos. I have learned that one must be brave or foolish to enter chaos. But that somewhere in chaos is art. The white light I didn't see. Chaos is sabotage. Chaos is not feminine. It is slovenly. But for me, it is the only place from which to create.

Audre Lorde, in a poem entitled "Syracuse Airport," writes that "women/ who take up space/ are called sloppy" (22). Making theatre, or any kind of art, is taking up space. It is not a lady-like thing to do. With your body, your voice, or your personal habits. The vast majority of my female acting students have soft and fey voices. This has nothing to do with incompetent vocal chords, and everything to do with the fear of taking up space, of being sloppy. Look at Jackie Kennedy, the American icon of feminine achievement, who spoke with the voice of a child: a strong and capable woman who did not wish to sound strong and capable.

Many girls cover their mouths when they laugh. Because laughter fills a space. All the physical mannerisms associated with girlishness are about repression and inhibition. Whatever encouragement our parents gave us, the culture hands us our pink girly masks at a very young age, and good, well-behaved girls wear them, as the self inside crumbles into dust or asserts itself in bizarre ways. My self asserted itself as a kind of quiet Lucille Ball, clumsy and absent-minded. At least this gave me an identity, and was a small act of sabotage. The next assertion was an act of unconscious revolution, the grand mal seizure that almost killed me.

And the next was *The Crackwalker*, my first play. And this is how I raged against the mask, and took up space in the world. And now, not surprisingly, I am seizure free.

***

I would like to discuss identity; that is, how my personal identity is affected by, and revealed in, the creation of dramatic character.

Although being a playwright has given me a reputation in my country and a strong public identity, the act of writing, or creating character, leaves me sometimes feeling that I have no identity at all. Every once in a while, when I am not writing or tending to my four children, I feel I am falling again down the terrible hole, with nothing to hold on to. And I believe this falling, this "identity panic," is a result of my using the very essence of myself to create character in dramatic work. I wonder sometimes if I am betraying my soul, by using its essence. However, I have found some comfort in the words of William Blake:

> Essence is not Identity, but from Essence proceeds Identity and from one Essence may proceed many Identities, as from one Affection may proceed many Thoughts.... If the Essence was the same as the Identity, there could be but one Identity, which is false. Heaven would upon this plan be but a clock; but one and the same Essence is therefore Essence and not Identity.[2]

Writing a play is for me, in the first few drafts, an act of faith. I enter a dark and dangerous forest of chaos, and I go where my instincts lead me, without a compass. I go get lost, essentially. So in many ways writing for me is like dreaming. There is no one in charge. Our dreams may be shocking and violent, highly erotic, or bizarre, but we do not hold ourselves responsible for our dreams. Our dreams happen to us. They are not who we have chosen to be in the world. But they are, as Native American culture has long recognized, who we truly are, as individuals, as members of a nation, and perhaps as members of the human race.

So I am written in my plays whether I want to be or not. My breath is the breath of the characters.

I often feel like I'm a character in a Grimms' fairy tale, as if with the creation of each character I cut off a piece of my body. A fingertip for this character, a toe for another, and on and on. I sometimes fear that eventually there will be no body left, only a ghost. The ghost is the old writer, who has finally given up her whole essence and therefore writes only parodies of what he or she used to write. I fear there is a heavy price to pay for the creation of a full-blooded character.

At a Writers' Guild Christmas party last December I questioned several writers about their thoughts on writing and identity. One of them told me that he found that the effect on his identity depends upon the nature of the project: if the project is commercial, such as, in his case, an episode he wrote for a sit-com called "Kung Fu," it has a serious, deleterious effect. He compared it to using one's furniture to keep a fireplace burning, and then afterwards being warm but with nothing left in the house. But when he works on something that matters to him, he said that rather than depleting the self, he found he discovered new areas of himself. I have certainly found this: I take great joy in the act of writing, and never find it painful—arduous, especially in the later drafts, but never painful. But somehow it doesn't seem to stop the feeling that there is a carving away of my essence, whatever that may be and however it can be defined (apart from genetics).

When I was in my twenties I read Aristotle's *Poetics*. I was very disturbed by his assertion that action was by far the most important part of a play, because character could only be defined by action. Until then, I had naively believed that character was defined by something the girls' magazines called "personality"—or public persona. Such and such a person was "nice" or "bubbly" or "shy" or "quick-tempered." This was who she was. What disturbed me most was that I knew Aristotle was right. And that meant that I was nobody. Because I was a suburban girl who had done nothing.

In my lower moments I attribute my ability to create a character to a lack of definition in myself, because to create a three-dimensional character a writer must, like an actor, become that character, or roam around inside that character. To do this one must be endlessly fluid and, in a sense, compromising. My first play, *The Crackwalker*, is about a man who, in a fit of despair, murders the child he loves. I did not have children when I wrote it. I cannot even watch it now, and when I must attend a performance out of courtesy, I plug my ears and close my eyes to the dreadful scene. When I wrote this scene, I did imagine myself to be this man, but I had to fake the baby part because I did not have children. I didn't even babysit. The reason the scene works is that, having just left an angry adolescence, I was able to understand his will to self-destruction.

One thing I often wonder about myself, given the demonic characters in so much of my work, is: how can I represent people I abhor? Am I so morally and ethically runny inside? And I wonder, if I give refuge in my soul to monstrous characters and then nurture them inside me, won't they make a monster of me? Isn't even the temporary experience of an evil impulse enough to damage me forever? Or is it perhaps an act of purification: to dig out and face the evil possibilities in oneself may be to cleanse oneself. To face the dark hole, to reach inside the bucket and pull out the rattlesnake and look it in the face; for me this is the act of creation. To face my greatest fears while not fully understanding them; to let the rattlesnake wrap itself around me and bite me, having faith that I will survive; to fall down that hole again knowing, knowing that I will find the light; this is, for me, what it is to write a play.

(1996)

Notes

[1] This essay is the text of a talk delivered by Judith Thompson at the Stratford Festival, 30 June 1996, as part of the Festival's Celebrated Writers Series.

[2] Thompson does not provide the source of this quotation (ed.).

Work Cited

Lorde, Audre. "Syracuse Airport." *The Marvelous Arithmetics of Distance (Poems 1987-1992)*. New York: Norton, 1993.

The Last Things in the Sled:
An Interview with Judith Thompson
by Jennifer Fletcher

On this sunny February day, Judith arrives by bicycle at the small café off Bathurst Street. She whirls into the bustling lunchroom to find Jennifer Fletcher sitting at a table by the window. Over a month has passed since the completion of the Tarragon's Public Workshop of her new play, Sled.

Jennifer Fletcher: How do you feel your script changed from the initial day of the workshop when it was called *Last Things*, to the final day when it emerged as *Sled*?

Judith Thompson: I don't feel it changed in essence, but I do feel that it basically lost fat and obstructions. Some people have said to me, "Oh you know, I'd love to see whatcha cut and you know make it longer." I have no problem with a seven-hour play. I wanted to have a long play but its natural length is what it is now. It's 2 hours and 40 minutes, without intermission, whereas most of my plays have been 1 hour and 45 minutes. So it's a long play. I really feel I have made the narrative stronger—more rhythmic. I took out any needless repetitions and needless information and reshaped scenes so that they rhythmically worked for the actors. I gave it shape. It went to the Y.

JF: The first draft of the play was very overtly political with respect to Native, francophone, and immigrant issues in Canada. The first draft of the Barbecue Dream scene[1] addressed a number of language issues with specific references to Native Canadians and French Canadians. The Eaton's scene illustrated the racism of a predominately Anglo–saxon Protestant Ontario with respect to Catholic Italian immigrants in the 1960s. With the cuts that you made to the script, including the deletion of the Barbecue Dream scene and the Eaton's scene in their entirety, do you feel that the politics of the play changed?

JT: Yes. It's interesting and I have said before that the Barbecue Dream scene is the politics of the play. In a sense it is the springboard of the play for me intellectually. When I send *Sled* to people to read, I always include the Barbecue Dream scene at the end. But we cut that, I cut that. You know the old adage: show, don't tell. It could never be better illustrated then in the progress and deletion of that scene. With a brilliant director, I could have made it work, but I cut it for two reasons. First, it is better to show rather than to tell and second, there is so much vulnerability to failure in that scene. This play will be done a lot over the years and ohhh I would hate to see some of the ... renditions of it—I mean it has the potential to be just frightening (*laughs*) and it sticks out like a sore thumb in the play.

JF: What do you feel was lost when you cut the Barbecue Dream scene? Or was anything lost?

JT: Well, this is what I fear. Perhaps I lost the idea of all the languages and the representation of the Toronto neighborhoods as being quite unique in the world. They are somewhat ghettoized but there's a lot of mixing happening, especially in the central area and what that means. I think I managed to maintain the languages in the top of the Pass Me The Sports Section scene. There was some Irish there and Jack speaks his Polish, and there are still the scenes with Italian.

JF: And the Norse which was placed into the scene where Kevin kills Annie.

JT: Yes, oh yes. Micky spoke the Norse so well. At the WHY THEATRE conference, I was interviewed by an American journalist and the Barbecue Dream scene is the one that I mentioned. That's the scene Nancy Palk would rave about when she talked about the play to people, yet she totally agrees with me that it had to go.

JF: The Barbecue Dream scene was also the scene that CBC recorded during the workshop.

JT: Oh yes. That was my choice.

JT: You mentioned before that you still include the Barbecue Dream scene when you send *Sled* out to be read.

JT: I don't know why I do that. I know it doesn't belong there, but it's my way of summarizing what I think the play is about.

JF: Did any of the feedback you received after or during the workshop from the audience influence any changes you made to the script?

JT: Mostly I completely disregard people's comments because they might not like something but they don't know why. They always offer reasons but they don't actually know why. One prominent writer who I respect very much offered some unsolicited advice. He loved most of *Sled* but he commented on a couple of things. He explained that he really loved the wilderness but had a problem going back to Joe in the city after the wilderness in the first act. I looked back at the script and I know that I can't go from the scene in the Pickerel Lodge restaurant where Jack forces Kevin to "learn some god damn respect," to the sensuous dance between Jack and Annie at the Lodge. Joe's "I used to have the satellite" scene, in between the two, is very important. It provides the counterpoint. I need it. Joe must be part of the play. Joe's turning into the past is a large part of the play. It's not obtrusive—it doesn't hurt the action. The same person also said that he didn't like Kevin's snowmobile and Northern Lights speech. He found the lyricism about "living in the green" which preceded the snowmobile speech to be so beautiful and striking that the snowmobile speech became too much. Here's how I took his two comments. I thought about what he said and I went back to the script. First, I looked at the snowmobile scene and I realized that the speech is important because Kevin's act is final. Kevin's speech is the biggest gift in the play and he gives it to Mike before Kevin kills him. If everything had gone all right for Kevin; he would have been the sports guy or the snowmobile guy. He would have headed up snowmobile associations. Even the language he uses sounds like it is borrowed from the senior sled guys, for example his line, "Nan-cy a-mazing lady." So we need that speech, but in the rehearsals I had lyricized it and changed it from the magazine-speak in which it was originally written. I thought I should lyricize it and I put a passage about the moon.

JF: Right.

JT: I had received a lot of good feedback for the change during rehearsals. Then I realized that writer's comments were right. That speech works better when it's very factoid. The only poetry should be, "the Northern Lights—Have you ever seen the Northern Lights?" The rest should be very, "We were up here, we were at the Bering Strait and this and that." It needed to have very little emotion so I cut out much of the emotion—almost all—and left just the line: "Have you ever seen the Northern Lights?"

That is the way I filtered the comments. I realized he wants to see more of the wilderness, but I can't remove Joe in the first act. He's just wrong about that. He doesn't understand about the narrative. However, I can bring back the wilderness at the end and it's probably very right. Therefore, I relocated the final scene from Joe's porch to the wilderness. That was the way I had it in the original draft before the workshop.

I have Kevin saying "It's so cold. It's so cold" and then Annie appears. The whole group is there and they see the moose. Kevin's mother, Diana, is there. I have Diana come back as the Mother because that's who she is most. It makes the most sense, doesn't it? Rather than the character of Essie returning. She gives him an apple and they all see this great moose. They follow the moose, presumably into the afterlife. Instead of the group watching the cows walk down the street from Joe's porch, they are now in a sense the cows walking down the street.

JF: What does Maurice Dean Wint's character come back as? In the last version of *Sled* he returned as Jason, Jack and Annie's son. Does he come back as Mike, Kevin's friend?

JT: Yes. He's Mike.

JF: Great!

JT: He's still Mike. He says, "oh yes, I've been down there," because he's been dead already.

So, *they* walk across the stage. They are the cows rather than seeing the cows. Now I've gotten rid of both those sort of stylized scenes, the Barbecue Dream scene and the Final Porch scene. It's better, the play needed those cuts. Those scenes, the Barbecue Dream and the Final Porch, were collisions. They didn't belong in that play. I'm very excited by those cuts.

JF: It's interesting that you changed the last scene too, because it seemed like the Barbecue Dream and the Final Porch scene were paired.

JT: They were. If the Barbecue Dream scene was there, the Porch scene would fit. Somehow the absurd quality of it works well on its own, but it doesn't belong in the play. That quality doesn't exist elsewhere in the script.

JF: Do you think the play changed stylistically, with respect to the deletion of the Barbecue Dream scene and the changes to the last scene—

JT: Even the Ambulance scene—there was a style to that—

JF: —Yes, the Ambulance scene was also cut. The original draft seemed to have many different styles, and then it moved more towards a naturalistic style.

JT: Yes. It's a, it's um, it's the magic realism. In a way it's like, as a writer I was trying to venture from the magic realism and naturalism but it's my style. Look at Michael Jordan. You know he went to baseball and he was okay at it, but he should play basketball. And I should stick to magic realism. It's what I love. It's what I love to watch and it's what I do best.

JF: Within the context of the workshop, do you think there were any other influences that pushed the script more towards a naturalistic style?

JT: I think it moved toward naturalism because naturalism is what emotionally engages me. The way I respond to what the actors are doing is very intuitive and visceral and physical. I can feel it in my body. I just, I love emotional naturalism. It's what moves me and it's what creates something that lives in you. I think it fortifies the ideas in the play and the themes that I would like people to go away and think about. You must to have emotional fortification. I think if it's just ideas, you walk away antsy. I know I do.

JF: What influenced you or helped you in making the changes?

JT: The truth in the acting and the quality of the acting. Because the acting was so good, I knew immediately when there was a problem with the text and not simply acting problems. If I had novice or amateur actors, I might as well have been working at my computer. It wasn't their suggestions—sometimes it was, but very rarely—it was their acting. I could watch Micky Mahonen make a bridge from this emotion to that emotion. I would know if I had to write another line or if I should cut a line. I could watch them making the leaps because they are such high calibre actors.

JF: How does the Tarragon theatre stand out in comparison to other theatres as a place to develop your scripts?

JT: I like the Tarragon. I like the size of the space, it's my favourite space with just two hundred seats. I think the space will work very well for *Sled*. *Lion in the Streets* was swallowed up by the ice house. It was my fault; being a relatively inexperienced director at that point I couldn't get them to fill the space—

JF: How do you feel this workshop compared with other ones you've done?

JT: We did one for *Crackwalker* (with Theatre Passe Muraille), *I Am Yours*, and *Lion in the Streets*. With *White Biting Dog* I just sat with Bill Glassco a lot. They were all good. Each one was better than the one before. The best was *Sled*. Having you and Scott [Duchesne, as script assistants] was the reason it was so good. I could do twice the amount of work. Going into the workshop, I knew that I would have assistants, so I wrote a much bigger play then I would have otherwise. I wouldn't have given myself so much work, if I hadn't known I would have an assistant. With all the help it was much easier to get it into shape.

JF: Especially when the printer was working *(laughs)*.

JT: *(Laughs)* Yeah. The public workshop was exhausting—I got ulcers after for two weeks. I can't tell you how depleted I felt after the workshop was over. I can't imagine what it would have been like if we had been fighting. It felt like I had been in a war and this one went so well!

(1996)

Note

[1] The "Barbecue Dream Scene," cut from the play, is published in Knowles, 12-16.

Work Cited

Knowles, Richard Paul [Ric]. "'Great Lines are a Dime a Dozen:' Judith Thompson's Greatest Cuts." *Canadian Theatre Review* 89 (Winter 1996): 8-18.

Inside Playwright Judith Thompson: Behind the Mask

by Andrew Vowles

"NO!" The scene is the rehearsal space in Lower Massey Hall at the University of Guelph. Monday, mid-morning. Outside the warped-glass windows, the first wet snow of the year drops like pebbles. Drama professor Judith Thompson is leading some 20 students in her Acting I class through their warm-ups. The students stand in a circle and take turns aiming a mock blow as they shout the word "No!" "More," she says to the less assertive. To others, whose "No!" sounds shredded, over the top, she holds up a hand: "More control." Thompson gestures to her diaphragm: "It has to come from here."

Scene: Thompson's Office, Massey Hall

On one wall hang pictures of actors engaged in a drama, mingled with children's school drawings. The desktop is practically bare. A black purse occupies one chair. A scarf has landed on the back of another. This is where the playwright hangs her hat during her classes and meets with students. She writes at home in Toronto's Annex neighbourhood, where she lives with her husband, Gregor Campbell, an English instructor at Guelph, and their five children: Ariane,13; Eli, 10; Grace, 8; Felicity, 4; and Sophia, 1.

Scene: University of Guelph Library Archives

Guelph Alumnus writer (Andrew Vowles): *(reading from draft of "Epilepsy and Snakes: Fear as the Genesis of Theatre," a talk given by Thompson to the Epilepsy Association of Metro Toronto in 1997. The script for the talk is included among boxes of correspondence, numerous drafts of plays, various newspaper and magazine articles, and reviews about the playwright and her work that Thompson recently donated to the U of G Library archives.)* I have known real fear only a few times in my relatively sheltered life. But I believe these moments of fear are directly connected to the source of creativity within me.

Scene: Just About Anywhere You Can Read a Play

Andrew Vowles: *(reading from introduction to Thompson's play* Sled, *which was first produced by Toronto's Tarragon Theatre in 1997)* Judith Thompson was born in 1954 in Montreal. She graduated from Queen's University in 1976, then graduated from the acting program of the National Theatre School in 1979. Although she worked briefly as a professional actor, she became more interested in writing, and at the age of 25, a workshop of her first script, *The Crackwalker*, was produced by Theatre Passe Muraille. Her work, which includes both radio and television writing, has enjoyed great international success.

Other plays include: *The Crackwalker, White Biting Dog, Pink, Tornado –* radio, *I Am Yours, Lion in the Streets, White Sand, Perfect Pie,* and *Stop Talking Like That*. She is the recipient of the Floyd S. Chalmers Canadian Play Award for *Lion in the Streets* in 1991 and *I Am Yours* in 1987, and the Governor General's Literary Award for Drama for *The Other Side of the Dark* in 1989 and *White Biting Dog* in 1984.

Scene: Lunchtime, University Club

Judith Thompson: I'm so grateful to have this job because it allows me to do the work that's important and the plays that will be my legacy and that they are what I feel I have to contribute to Canadian culture. If I didn't have this job, I'd have to keep compromising because my plays don't make money. They're always in smaller houses, I take chances, they're not commercial. They play all over the world, but always in smaller places. I would just have to pursue life as a Screenwriter to make a living .... This job gives me the great privilege of doing my research, which is the plays that I write and the editorial work that I sometimes do and screenplays that are worthy and good projects.

AV: Audiences and reviewers have described your plays as dark, disturbing, full of angry people, full of profanity ...

JT: At the risk of sounding grandiose, I seem to give voice to people who have no voice or very little in the culture, whom people don't listen to. *Lion in the Streets*, the handicapped woman living in the basement all on her own, the young girl, Isobel. The secretary stuck in this abusive relationship with the actor. The middle-class housewife dumped by her husband because he doesn't like her sweatsuits and on and on. I give voice to them because, I don't know, because I care about them, because I like to represent them. I'm a lawyer. Some of them use profanity because they have really good reason to be angry and most of them are powerless. And unfortunately, profanity has a little charge. It's a little source of baby power. It upsets me, I don't use it myself, I'm very sensitive to it.

Scene: Archives

AV: (*reading essay by Thompson commissioned by Toronto literary journal* Brick *in 1995*) If I were not a writer, I think I would wear a riding hat. With a steel lining. Because I would be having many more epileptic seizures than I do presently. Because any of the non-writer real jobs I have had caused me sleepless nights, self-disgust, swollen eyes, cystic acne and hearing disorders, all of which increased electrical activity in my brain, which, I believe, increases the frequency of seizures.

Scene: University Club

JT: (*discussing the critical and public reaction to her first play,* The Crackwalker) It was slaughtered at first, as all my plays have been. Very bad reviews at first, and them somehow they catch fire and there's one great review and the others start to see something.

AV: Why the bad reviews?

JT: I think people might say that they're shocking, but I don't think so, not with the movies we see and whatnot. They're not shocking compared with Quentin Tarantino. But they're not like anything else; they don't know where to put them. And when they don't know where to put them, they're dismayed, I think, and hostile, and they feel challenged. I just write as I see. I'm not trying to shock or challenge anyone. I hope they do challenge—me too, all of us. I often feel like the little boy in *The Emperor's New Clothes*: Look, this is what I see.

Scene: Lower Massey Hall

Two "Acting I" students perform a scene on the stage. Their fellow students sit on the floor, watching. Thompson sits forward on a plastic chair, forearms propped on her knees, hands clasped before her. Her eyes, her body, are intent on the action.

Later …

Amberley Buxton: (*first-year student in Acting I, who is pursuing a psychology major and a drama minor*) It's a really intense class. In one of our first classes, we were to share something that had changed our perspective on life or how we thought every day. Later during improvisation or scene work, she had us draw on the emotional context from those stories to add to our acting experiences. It's really intense in that way. A lot of people share a lot of personal things, and we use each other's experiences.

Scene: University Club

JT: Each semester, students go through an intensive transition. In order to find your creative centre or trigger, you need to know yourself in an intellectual context. They reach that place and find their genius. My philosophy is that every student has genius, and it's my job to uncover it …. My relationship is so intense with students. The classes are very psychoanalytic. It seems to transform their life.

Scene: Lower Massey

AB: Even if we haven't encountered a similar situation in real life, she has us draw on something similar. For our exam, I'm doing a monologue. My character has been abused. I haven't been abused myself, but I have to draw on a situation where I had similar feelings, draw on some experience. Like being teased at school. Even something as small as that, if you find a way to get back to that…

Scene: University Club

JT: I used to be terrified. In high school, I'd spend half my time in the nurse's room because the idea of having a seizure in front of your peers at that age was just petrifying. I did finally have a seizure, but luckily no one was around at the time. So I think all of that puts me in touch with a lot in life I might not have been in touch with, being fairly privileged, not rich, but enough to be middle class. A lot of my work is about class, about the class differentiation in Canada. I've somehow felt more allied to a less advantaged class …. My grandfather once sat as prime minister of Australia. My grandfather on the other side was a member of the Royal Society, an entomologist, but his mother died in childbirth and he was brought up as a cousin on the farm outside of London. And my Australian grandfather was one of eleven siblings in a shack by the side of the railroad. His father had died. He walked barefoot to school, so I think because it's just two generations away, I feel it in my bones and my blood.

AV: How did you get to writing?

JT: Through acting. I've been involved in theatre since I was 11 years old. I was Helen Keller for a university show my mother directed. She had an MA in theatre and she taught it at Queen's. I was in *The Crucible* when I was 12 in Kingston and *Jean Brodie* and on and on and on. I would just listen to all these wonderful lines and words, and it all kind of entered me. And acting is where I really found my niche as a person. The theatre became my home. Then I went to theatre school as an actress, but I started to create mask characters through improvisation. That's where I really took off in a big way and where I found myself very, very excited.

AV: What were you excited about?

JT: I was doing the writing. And I felt frankly that I did it much better than most of the texts I was working with. Not Shakespeare, but … and it's not a matter of better, it's … that's where I belonged. So I would go home and write down the characters that I created that day in class and make them talk to each other, and that's how *The Crackwalker* happened.

I spent a summer in Toronto looking for acting work and I got a few jobs. But every day for a couple of hours, I would write at a typewriter, and I found these voices coming. At the end of it, I said to someone: You know, I think this isn't bad, I think this might even be a play. At the National Theatre School, they said to me: You're pretty handy with these monologues, but don't ever think you could write a play. (*Pause.*) I enjoy telling that tale on them.

Scene: Lower Massey

AB: It was my first time doing mask work. She had us sit with the masks on and just stare at ourselves in the mirror. We did it for an hour, staring at the mask, feeling the mask. It was a phenomenal experience, the way you're able to transform yourself. It was almost as if you weren't looking at you. That helped you to walk differently. You were able to shed your own movements and personality.

Scene: University Club

JT: I think that seizures can translate into creativity, are part of me as a creative artist. People in the medical business are very skeptical of anything like this. But I feel it's because I have fewer inhibitors in my brain …. You have these inhibitors, and that's what medication helps. But if you're epileptic, your inhibitors aren't working as well to put out the electrical fire, so it spreads. I think the door to my unconscious is kind of flapping around, so I think that helps creatively.

Scene: Massey Hall

Student: (*stepping forward*) NO!

JT: (*quietly*) Good.

Scene: Archives

AV: (*reading from "Epilepsy & the Snake"*) I have no doubt that my experience with epilepsy has contributed to my creative work, partly because it helped me to understand what it is to be marginalized, to be isolated, to be fearful, and to be out of control, and even to be mortal …

Scene: University Club

JT: Unchecked id can mean scrawling on the walls, crazy things, muttering in street corners, because they're all id, no superego. But I had the luck to be born into a theatrical family, my mother having the theatrical experience, so I was exposed to it. Lots of books. I was taken to a lot of plays. Having epilepsy, my first seizure when I was nine, I was able to link with that. If I hadn't had those advantages, who knows, the seizures might have just made me a depressed person, an angry person. And you're touched with mortality, you always live under siege, a slight fear of having a seizure. It's much less so now with me.

Scene: University Club

JT: I've always been a mimic in a cheap way. I could always mimic well. I would talk to someone on a bus and I could do them exactly. That's kind of dangerous because it can be pretty shallow. But it showed me a way into the person through voice. And once I could do that, like a puppet, something would click and I could get in in a deeper way.

I need to get so thoroughly into the characters and their state of mind and especially tapping repressed emotion, which gets you in touch with your id or unconscious life. If one character is about rage, I have to tap into my own rage, and that's why the monologues, So things can just flow and then I can retrieve things from the past and remember things. So it's not working from here (*gestures to midriff*), its working from here (*gestures to head*).

Monologues for me are always the key to finding out who the character is, because if you can't make them rant for five minutes, you don't know them. That's what I tell my playwriting students. I want to see two pages of this character's mouth. In other words, to speak for five minutes, we have to have something to say. We have to have something we feel passionately about, something we're angry about, and if we don't have something to say for five minutes, who are we?

Scene: University Club

AV: Where do you see what eventually becomes a play such as *Sled*?

JT: I was at a lodge and saw a moose, that's one thing. And that made me think about winter and how the country is always with us as Canadians. Even in the urban centres, we carry it with us. There's always this seeming division between the country, the wilderness and civilized centres, but it's the same. The wildness of the moose and the hunt and the bear is in our neighbourhoods. I guess it's like *Lion in the Streets*, it must be a thing with me. And also the exquisite beauty, and that's how most of the world thinks of Canada, as the wilderness. It's not quite how we think of ourselves, but it is partly. So that made me want to do something about the North, violence in the North.

As far as the old man's stories, that was my neighbour and he told me all those stories, they were all true, except maybe one or so, and I thought, "They're amazing." They tell us what our neighbourhoods are really about and Toronto, what the city is, how it's constructed. Toronto is our stories, and in these neighbourhoods you have an urbane entertainer living next to an 80-year-old Italian man, and that's the beauty of Toronto, and it's the way the world is changing. The strict class divisions and culture divisions, they're no longer as defined as they were, especially in these neighbourhoods, the great pioneering experiment.

AV: Do your children see your work?

JT: No. None of my children can see my plays. Ariane saw *I Am Yours* in New York when she was about nine. I do deal with the dark and what's true, and my children aren't ready for that. I'm probably more protective than most mothers. Walk them to school till they're 13, that kind of thing.

AV: You were interviewed in *The Globe and Mail* recently in a story about motherhood and the muse. How do you handle the demands of motherhood and writing?

JT: If I'm in the situation where I have 15 or so hours of child care a week, I'm okay because when I'm with them, I want to be with them, and when I'm doing my work, that's what I do. But if I do something like a workout, then a black cloud descends. The guilt and the black cloud that descend as I take off on my bike, it's huge. Then once the workout's finished, I know it was a good thing to do, although it's also cut into my work time. I do feel guilty about the nature of my work, too, in that my kids can't see it. Am I drawing on a part of me that's not good as a mother? The other part of me is that I make up bedtime stories and bake cookies and all that stuff. I'm probably a rather operatic mother. I cry at movies, laugh too hard …

Scene: Archives

AV: (*reading from "Epilepsy & the Snake"*) Although being a dramatic writer has given me a reputation in my country and a strong identity, the act of writing or creating character leaves me sometimes feeling that I have no identity at all. Every once in a while, when I am not writing or tending to my four children, I feel I am falling again down the terrible hole, with nothing to hold on to. And I believe this falling, this "identity pain," is a result of me using the very essence of myself to create character in a dramatic work. I wonder sometimes if I am betraying my soul, in a way, by using its essence. However, I have found some comfort in the words of William Blake: "Essence is not Identity, but from Essence proceeds Identity, and from one Essence may proceed many Identities, as from one Affection may proceed many thoughts .... If the Essence was the same as the Identity, there could be but one Identity, which is false. Heaven would upon this plan be but a clock; but one and the same Essence is therefore Essence and not Identity."

Scene: University Club

JT: I always put myself in a play and never. In other words, I take little sections of myself and grow them in a petri dish of the play. So if I've found a moment where I'm a bit lazy, I'll grow it and make the character very lazy or impatient or whatever. So I take these moments, because we all have all of them, grow them and create this Frankenstein's monster, a character right out of parts, body parts and psychological parts, often of myself, and then observe things in other people, but I have to find it in myself to make it work.

Scene: Archives

JT: *(reading from "Epilepsy & the Snake")* My self asserted itself as a kind of quiet Lucille Ball, clumsy and absent-minded. At least this gave me an identity and was a small act of sabotage. The next assertion was an act of unconscious revolution, the grand mal seizure that almost killed me. And the next one was *The Crackwalker*, my first play. And this is how I raged against the machine and took space in the world. And now, not surprisingly, I am seizure-free.

Scene: Lower Massey

After another pair of actors runs through their scene, Thompson directs them to begin again. She interrupts frequently to question the students about actions, feelings, motivations. At one point, as the Students pause to consider her words, Thompson turns to the rest of the class, erect in her chair.

JT: Isolate the moment. The great thing about the stage is that it isolates the moments that just race by us.

Scene: University Club

JT: I've just written my next play, which is not called *Perfect Pie*, but that's its working title because it came from a monologue called "Perfect Pie." But now it's a full two-hour play in which the second woman comes back and then I have them as young girls, too. It goes back and forth, and it's very exciting. I workshopped it in the spring and in December at the Tarragon and it will go on in one year. At the same time, I'm writing a feature film for Rhombus based on the play *Perfect Pie*.

Scene: University Club

JT: My plays are musically written. And if somebody doesn't get the music, they don't feel it and go with the rhythms, it throws the whole thing off. I hear the plays, I hear them, I write with my ear. They change a lot, but it's according to rhythm. I'll be sitting in rehearsal listening and if it doesn't sound right, I change it so that it's rhythmic.

Scene: Just About Anywhere You Can Read a Play

AV: (*reading from the script of* White Biting Dog, *first produced at the Tarragon Theatre in 1984*) Because of the extreme and deliberate musicality of this play, any attempts to go against the textual rhythms, such as the breaking up of an unbroken sentence, the taking of a pause where none is written in, are DISASTROUS. The effect is like being in a small plane and suddenly turning off the ignition. It all falls down. This play must SPIN, not just turn around.

Scene: Lower Massey

Her students listen as Thompson stands to complete a soliloquy about capturing the rhythm of the language on the stage. The wide sleeves of her ankle-length dress slide down her forearms as she gestures.

JT: Listen to the music of the scene. Each playwright writes their own symphony.

Scene: University Club

JT: I've been pretty directed to this from an early age, although if I had done anything else, it probably would have been some form of social work. I would have been smoking three packs of cigarettes a day and working in an office somewhere up in Scarborough.

Scene: Archives

AV: (*reading from* Brick *interview of Thompson by Eleanor Wachtel, 1991*) In the theatre, I think what one must do is confront the truth, confront the emotional truth of our lives, which is mired in the swamp of minutiae, everyday minutiae. Maybe it has to be that way, because we couldn't confront it every day. But I think the theatre must. I'm not interested in theatre that doesn't.

(1999)

Turning an Elephant into a Microphone:
A Conversation on Translation and Adaptation
by Judith Thompson, edited by Ric Knowles

Excerpts from Judith Thompson's contributions to a panel discussion about the complexities of translating and adapting for the stage. The panel, chaired by George Elliot Clarke, was held on 18 October, 2002, as part of the Celebrating Canadian Plays and Playwrights Conference at the Stratford Festival. A transcript of the panel was edited by Ric Knowles.

I have four experiences that I can speak about. The first was an adaptation of *Hedda Gabler* I did for the Shaw Festival.[1] I took five or six existing translations plus a lot of the early drafts, and then adapted the text. The next was *Motel Hélène*, a Serge Boucher play that I adapted from a literal translation by Morwyn Brebner. There are some really interesting issues that came up there, especially the issue of swearing. I wasn't going to pretend that this group of people living outside of Montreal was a group of southern Ontario folk, because there's a completely different culture. So I thought the only way that I could do that was to hang on to the swear words, which are really symptomatic of how different the cultures are. All of our swear words are anti-sex, and all about the body, and all the Québécois swear words then, at the time of the play, were all around the Catholic religion. So I kept the swear words in French. Translation is never smooth, it's never complete, it's always problematic, and you're only seeing about a third of what the play really is. You're sort of pointing to the play, although the heart of *Motel Hélène* did survive, with wonderful acting and everything.

Then there's adapting for film. I adapted a book of Susan Swan's, *The Wives of Bath*, for film, which was quite radically different, but I think she felt I kept the heart of it. And I've just adapted my own play, *Perfect Pie*, for film. So four very different experiences and always the work in translation or adaptation becomes a different creature.

***

Right before 9-11 there was a whole Québec culture program in New York and *Motel Hélène* was going to have a staged reading at the Public [Theatre], and we met with the director and a few of the other people involved. But Serge got nervous about the American reception of the piece, and demanded that I make the swearing English and bring more of an English, southern Ontario *Crackwalker* style to it. But I couldn't, because I really felt I was betraying his text, which

I really loved. So we had to part ways—in a friendly way of course. I just said, "You'll have to do it. I can't do it because it's not the same play to me."

***

I just thought about cereal boxes. We live in a culture that's based on the hope that translation is possible and easy and fluid, but in many ways that's not true. When you look at some of the translations on cereal boxes and start to understand them, you find that they're absurd. I think of one of the lines in Serge's play: when a character said that when he was rejected by his lover he felt like an earthworm curled in the sand, a crying earthworm upside down in the sand. That's just impossible in English, so I had to just make this flying leap and I couldn't withhold my voice. I wanted to. You want to just be a neutral mask, be a good citizen, do an accurate translation, but my stinky voice just comes in and spreads all over the page. So maybe it's not good to employ a playwright to translate. Someone neutered needs to do translations. I wonder if surtitles wouldn't be better, because you hear the flow of the original.

***

You're drawing on the same source then, not translating or adapting. It's a re-creation. But I wouldn't "translate" any of my plays to film again because the whole motivation is suspect in that process—the film is somehow more glamorous, more glorious, and involves more money. It reaches more people, but I think it is an act of violence to a play, because I think as playwrights we conceive a work as a play the way a poet conceives a poem as a poem, and to make a poem into a film— I guess you could, but you'd be turning an elephant into a microphone.

***

We know as playwrights—every one of us in this room who's a playwright knows—that the dialogue doesn't just service the action. In many plays the dialogue can *be* the action. It is the medium, and when you translate, that whole layer is removed. Some plays can survive it and some can't.

***

You have to go to the physical state that Paul Thompson was talking about [on an earlier panel] comparable to the way an actor feels an impulse in their body. That's what the playwright does too, and you have to get in character and go to where that playwright went. Go right back to the source impulse and then see how it comes out in your language.

***

Regarding topical references, I think that all of us as Canadian playwrights, as we write and hope for productions across the US, we unconsciously or semi-consciously adapt our own work and often remove—or have a conversation with ourselves about removing—specific cultural references, Canadian references. I definitely have, because they don't want them there. You have a greater chance of being produced across the United States if you cut or change them. And yet I feel I'm betraying where I live, who I am, what this country is becoming if I do erase those references. So I think that this adaptation/translation goes on within a single language as well.

***

Audience Member: Judith, could you talk a little bit about your *Hedda Gabler*, what you did and why you did it?

JT: Yeah, why did I do it? I looked back on it when I saw a production in Ottawa and I thought, "It's so short! I must have been really impatient when I was doing it." And I know it was, as somebody there said at the time, *Hedda Gabler* on rollerblades. So I'm a bit angry at myself now. I would add twenty minutes to it now. But I did the adaptation because I just wanted to immerse myself in—I'm, you know, a closet classicist—I wanted to immerse myself in that play and know it from the inside out. It's an important play, and it tells us a lot about the sociopolitical history of the times. I wanted to get deeply inside it.

Audience Member: So you didn't feel any obligation to respect the authoritative text, or the published text.

JT: When I look back on it I wish they'd leaned on me more. They gave me complete freedom.

***

Gerd Hauck: I recently did an adaptation of *Miss Julie*, using about eight English texts, and German and Swedish versions. But unfortunately, *Miss Julie* is flawed. It's not a perfectly written play. There are some passages that are very, very unclear, especially Jean's passages when he is attempting to speak in an upper-class language. I was wondering how you deal with that? Because if you render it accurately in English it sounds really, really bad. When something is flawed in the original, how do you deal with that?

JT: I think it's something anybody who works on a biography deals with. Suddenly, in this person you worshipped, you see flaws, and you hate them and you love them. In Ibsen I saw where there were flaws too, but it's not up to me to fix them. How did you approach it?

GH: I made it sound as if it was normal English, and that was the best I could do. But you're actually doing a disservice to the original.

***

Audience member: Judith, you did the screenplay for *Perfect Pie*, but the play was a separate creation. As the writer of both, would you be willing to say a little bit about the relationship between the play and the film?

JT: Sure. The story found its form as a play. It was originally a long monologue, and I was turning it into a play, and then I was commissioned to do the screenplay. So the finishing of the screenplay was very much informed by finding the story in the form of a play, because I conceive stories through voices. It was a terrible struggle, and I'd never do it again. All the elements that drove the piece—the Irish-Protestant divide, the persecution of Irish-Catholics by Orangemen in Ontario, my own epilepsy, the gang rape—were going to be cut out of it. It was difficult, because film's such a director's medium, and they want their vision to be realized. They start actually thinking it's their own story you know? "When I was a little girl, because of my interest in classical music I felt persecuted too"—but it's not really the same. It's just not the same. It's a beautiful movie, but there are essential clashes and problems that I can still see.

(2003)

Note

[1] The adaptation referred to here and discussed below was produced at the Shaw Festival in 1991. Thompson has since "re-adapted" the play for production by Volcano Theatre at Buddies in Bad Times, Toronto, in Spring 2005.

"I Will Tear You to Pieces": The Classroom as Theatre
by Judith Thompson

When I was eleven years old, I became Helen Keller. As I rehearsed the role for the amateur production, I felt I was, for the first time, vivid; the caul that seemed to always surround me slipped away while I explored this desperate, mythic character. I had been largely an invisible child with no opinions or even thoughts of my own; I lived by sensation. From that time I remember the purple of violets, the yellow of buttercups, and the cherry of Popsicles, suffocating. New England summer afternoons, dirty feet, and dark chocolate cake against deep green grass, these sensations were like hands in soft clay; I had, as a child, the constant and overwhelming sensation of being excluded from the world, of living in somebody's dream; the child who met the outside world was faceless and voiceless, and so I was typecast, in a way, as a girl who was blind, deaf, and dumb. I felt pure, dizzying joy and freedom being on stage, screaming and throwing the forks and knives to the floor; snorting like a pig, writhing and moaning, clutching the sweaty hand of the faculty wife who played Annie, the teacher. Her hand became my whole world during that time, the hand was language, my door to the outside world and my protection from it; the hand that smelled so strongly of sweat and metals; I was not surprised to find out many years later that the actress had died of liver cancer. In some ways, this role was the template for my role as a dramatist, and as a teacher.

My next big theatrical role/moment was *The Grand Mal Seizure*. I was graduating from grade six at Stillman School in Middletown, Connecticut—"We wish we could stay at Stillman School for E-E-E ver"—and I was wearing my carefully ironed pink linen dress, sitting in assembly with every student in the school from kindergarten through grade six. I suddenly felt a sharp evil pain in my stomach, whispered to a friend that the worms in the film about fishing were going to make me faint, and then fell to the floor convulsing in a tonic-clonic seizure for the whole school to see. In this seizure, there was, again, a horrible kind of freedom; not only was I free to scream, I had to scream to save my life, to breathe; my face turned purple and I became incontinent; my dress was soaked in front of every student in the school. They watched, and of course snickered as I grunted and convulsed and struggled for life.

The seizure had the force of a great volcano erupting, the bubbling, white hot lava trammelling over the fragile, spindly structures that make up a conscious self.

My next role, at the Domino Theatre in Kingston, Ontario, was Betty, in Arthur Miller's *The Crucible*. I remember auditions well—the possibility that there was a way out of day-to-day existence in a Loyalist university town with nine federal prisons within the city limits. Of course I did not know this at the time; all I knew was my new street, which still smelled of sawdust and oil paint. And my school, St Thomas More, was full of tough-talking Catholic kids whose southern Ontario drawl I had learned immediately, as a matter of survival, to deftly imitate. As soon as I stepped into the musty dark theatre and sat and read a script, there was that rush again. The rush that I would live for. I was given the role and my life in the theatre truly began. These were seasoned amateur actors, the best in the city; many of them could have been professional, some of them are now. The production went to the Sears Drama festival, and won awards. It was the most thrilling time in my young life; in fact, it was the first time I knew what thrill was.

As Betty Parris, I was allowed to scream the scream to end all screams. Years of rage, and of feeling invisible came out in that scream. I was told that pregnant women had to leave the theatre. I would lie on the stage bed in the first act, and listen to all that exquisite, musical language and then try to fly—"Mama, Mama, I want to fly to MAMA"—and scream until I passed out.

Every time I sit down to write, to create a drama, I feel that I am again playing Helen Keller and Betty Parris; I am in the assembly, surrendering to the nuclear power of a seizure. I am deaf, dumb, and blind and I am screaming: free to have tantrums, to groan and grunt and foam at the mouth and bite and be an animal, and to fly. I am screaming to save my life.

I have no sense of decorum or structure. I have no control, no idea of what I am going to write, only faith in my fingers, for the play lies in them, just as Helen met the world through her fingers. Touch is all. Betty Parris is in a trance just as I am, she believes she can fly, she believes she is the devil just as I believe I am in the play I am writing, and I am all the characters. To write, I have to become, basically, a child who is a wild animal.

The rest of the time, I am an ordinary, rather slow-witted but good-humoured woman, the kind of mother who falls asleep in front of CBC documentaries at ten fifteen every night, and does two loads of laundry before waking the kids at eight in the morning.

It's when I enter the sphere of drama that I become Helen and Betty again. And teaching drama, of course, means entering that sphere.

Since my first professional production, of *The Crackwalker*, in 1979 at Theatre Passe Muraille, I had taught here and there: a few night classes, a few workshops, and many readings followed by animated discussions with students, but I had never thought of myself as a Teacher. I was a playwright who, I had naïvely thought, could just continue to live on small grants and smaller royalties, the occasional job with the CBC, making about twelve thousand dollars a year. And as a childless artist I could have, but as I began to have children, a choice that was a spiritual imperative for me, it became apparent that we would need a reliable source of income.

When I was first offered a tenure-track teaching job at Guelph, I was nonplussed. I somehow did not see clearly what a tremendous coup this was, and how it would save my life as a playwright and as a mother. For this is one of the only institutions that values artistic work enough to actually pay us to do it.

Sadly, I shared the bias against teaching that many of my colleagues in the theatre have, believing teaching to be something one does for financial reasons only. It was, I thought, something of an admission of failure. Many of my colleagues actually said, "Oh you won't stay there long," and when I was finding it stressful, advised me to quit. Every day I thought about quitting.

I am so thankful that I didn't.

Not only because working at the university allows me to continue to write for the stage, which I would not be able to do if I were frantically pursuing film and television gigs to support my family, but because every class is the creation of a new drama. And aside from my children, and the occasional blissful walk through a park, or bite of fresh hot bread, that is where I find pure joy.

When I first started to teach, I had stage fright. I was floundering and improvising; I am shy in a profoundly visceral way, and found the scrutiny of the students excruciating. Because of self-esteem problems rooted in childhood, I found it impossible to think of myself as any kind of expert, even though my success and experience in the field of theatre should have persuaded me that I knew something. Politically, I found the idea of The Teacher as Regent to be abhorrent. I had a few vague ideas about thwarting the pedagogical model of expertise and paternalism, but I wasn't sure what I would replace it with. I had hoped the students would just have faith, as the theatre practitioners who worked with me did. I had hoped we would discover together. What I hadn't realized is that many of the students, schooled in our tired, bureaucratic system, wanted me to perform the role of "teacher"; they wanted a strong hand, an expert who would firmly guide them, give them a little book of rules, so that they wouldn't have to think for themselves. But I refused to play along. I blithely told them that I knew nothing. There were no rules. The only rule was to leap, and to trust what came out. A few of them were excited by this, but most of them were perplexed. I tried to teach them about leaping, and trusting one's deeper, rawer instincts and one's life stories. But it was like one of those wrenching roller-coaster love affairs; one day would be wonderful, the next terrible.

At the end of the first semester, I received a couple of evaluations so filled with hate it shocked me. One said that I was completely unapproachable, while the next in the pile said I was very approachable. And although there were already quite a few who were very positive, it seemed to me that the majority found me "disorganized." A couple of students complained to my Chair that they were not learning anything. He told them to listen harder, and accept that my teaching style was unique. What they called disorganization, I called flexibility, immediacy, and fluidity. Much of our learning culture is a stale leftover of the British military model, and Canadians traditionally have always preferred the precise, hierarchical, rule-centred approach to learning.

I began to hate and fear teaching. I started to arrive a little later every day, and feel huge relief when the class was over. When I was away from the university I tried to forget the existence of the students. A few of them, whom I found threatening because they were resisting my approach and aggressively arguing with all my choices, began to take over my psychic landscape. Their faces would invade my pre-sleep cinema, filling the screen, moving closer, suffocating me. I never slept the night before a teaching day, and therefore found myself so exhausted I would have to fight sleep even while I taught. I wanted to quit, but I was not in a financial position to do so. So I was forced to find a way to make the classroom work.

It was like the moment in my worst seizure, when I was fifteen, when I felt I was at the middle of the earth; I knew that I was about to die, and if I didn't want to die I would have to somehow find a way to breathe, and to scream, to scream myself out of the earth and into the air, and life, and a future. Through sheer will I breathed, deeply, and I screamed so loud that the principal came running out of the school, scolding me for disturbing people.

My transformation into a good teacher began with a deep breath, which enabled me to see clearly what I needed to do. The first step, of course, was what I, as an artist who valued immediacy so highly, had ignored: basic organization— a watch and a day book—clearly symbolic outward signs of commitment to the art of teaching. Next, I convinced myself that teaching and artistic practice are not mutually exclusive, but that one could in fact be a necessity for the other.

Second, I accepted that yes, of course, I was qualified to teach about the theatre; that I had in fact a great deal of experience in the theatre, and a mine of knowledge about the art and craft of theatre that could be of tremendous value to the students. I did not stumble into my success through sheer dumb luck. I actually did know something about my discipline that I could pass on. If that mantra sounds only half-convincing, it is because I am still working on convincing myself of it. Some days I walk in believing it all, and some days, well, I am just not so sure.

Perhaps that uncertainty exists because I do believe that when a play is successful, as a piece of writing, it is because I have allowed the under-belly of the culture I live in to reveal itself through the play. I have shaped the play, using my craft, so that certain hidden truths, about who we are, are illuminated. And "rules of dramatic writing" are the last thing on my mind when I am creating a new play. This is why I do not teach them rules, but rather sensibility.

The most important epiphany for me may sound like something out of a dime-store self-help book: I realized that if I truly valued the students, they would value me. For somehow, mixed in with my low self-esteem, there was a certain arrogance—which came from the general attitude in the theatre towards teaching. I liked working with my peers, artists who would take chances and question all traditional methods of discovery and hierarchy, not with some cocky high school kid from Whitby whose sole exposure to the theatre was the school musical, and who might be sniggering about me behind my back or talking all the way through class. I finally accepted that I had something to learn from that ordinary girl in the back row from Brampton. Instead of looking at teaching her as an eye-rollingly tedious task, I came to understand that the idea of talent is a Hollywood invention, and a form of élitism; in fact, every person in the world has talent, because there is pure genius in each person, a universe in every soul, and now I always approach my first class with this idea. Indeed, I do witness a moment of genius from every student. And even if it is only a moment, the knowledge that they have this genius changes students forever.

My standards are high, and I treat the classroom as a rehearsal hall. Punctuality, respect, and concentration are all important. And now my evaluations are overwhelmingly positive. I am still frightened to read them, always fearing the bad review—but I have been pleasantly surprised since the second or third semester.

Thus, teaching is like writing a play. If I write from an idea about writing, or structure; if I write something I am assigned to write that I am not very excited about; if I write with a view to getting it over with, getting the paycheck; and if I do not have blood on every page, I do slovenly work. But if I write from my deepest self, with strength and raw passion, with respect for my characters and the structure they dictate, I have a play, and I have a classroom. Teaching drama is, in fact, writing drama. A class can only succeed if the dramatist, or teacher, makes the right choices. Are the most dramatic choices always the right choices? And is it possible that a dramatist of my sensibility can make dangerous choices as a teacher? choices that, like high diving, can produce either spectacular results or, possibly, tragic accidents?

Some theorists, such as Keith Johnstone, claim that all theatre is about power. Within the classroom the power dynamic is inherently theatrical; it seems to be set in steel—Teacher as Regent and Students as Peasants—but in actuality it shifts and changes. Sometimes I can feel certain individuals resisting my efforts to communicate in an egalitarian way, trying to force me into a mythical teacher role, or objectifying me. I try to communicate with them until they are forced to see me as a human being, and not as "teacher mask." We are discovering together, and everything that happens in the class is a collective creation. But in the end, however deeply we communicate, and however much I respect them, I will be giving them a grade. This makes me a threat. This makes me the enemy.

Because I encourage students to use the classes and the exercises to find themselves and reveal themselves, because I believe that the writing of a play is the writing of the self, and the acting of the role is the acting of a deeper and invisible part of the self, there may be a few students who find and reveal a self that makes for great drama, but in the real world is frightening and dangerous.

This unavoidable reality makes the classroom deeply Shakespearean. I am the Queen who never wanted to be queen, and, like Hermione in *A Winter's Tale*, sometimes standing accused of crimes (too strict, unapproachable, plays favourites) of which I know I am innocent.

The reality is, no matter how nice the boss is, everyone resents their boss, and most people, at one time or another, hate their boss. Because we hate it that people can be more powerful than we are; we hate for our future to be in their hands. In students who are somewhat emotionally unstable, a psychological transference occurs. And although this usually is revealed in the form of a positive focus, sometimes it is extremely negative. I think the power dynamic will always disturb me. I live in fear of being corrupted by it, in the sense of believing too much in my own power and expertise, of becoming complacent, like so many teachers before me.

Sometimes, out of this theatre of power in the classroom arises a harrowing drama.

He was from a small northern Ontario town, and apparently he was king of the bar crowd there. He had a big voice with a strong northern Ontario accent and his language was full of hilarious and vulgar regional idioms. He was elfish-looking, prematurely bald, and chubby with small hands, with a fire in his eyes that was sometimes mistaken for a twinkle. He was an incandescent presence in the classroom and on the stage. He was compelling in the manner of a hypnotic union leader, with an authority and a charm that could persuade the listener that what they thought was right was wrong, what they thought was red was blue. When he cracked a joke, everyone laughed, no matter how lewd or violent. Once he told a story from his childhood about the brutal beating of another boy for the sole reason that he and his buddies didn't like the boy's pants, and he had the whole class chuckling. I confess even I had to resist the urge to chuckle: this urge came from his charm alone, not from the words I was hearing, because the words he was uttering were the words of a violent bully. He was proud of what he had done. There was not a hint of any kind of regret. He had broken the victim's jaw and nose. He was excited by the blood. And all the other students, who for the most part were progressive, deeply emotional, and giving individuals, were grinning like fools. He looked at me when he finished the story, expecting to be scolded. All I said was "That was an excellent story; it tells us a lot about our culture." Yet inwardly I marvelled at the power of theatre, of propaganda. From the very first class I noticed that, in contrast to the openness of the rest of the students, his eyes were veiled when he addressed me. For some reason, he had decided that I was the enemy.

Perhaps he did not like my gay-positive, feminist sensibility; perhaps he just did not like me. He was the kind of person who could find someone's weakness immediately, and it was almost as if he could see through my success and authority to the shy girl who had pennies thrown at her in grade eleven because her acne was so bad, the incompetent waitress who was fired several times, the girl who had always felt ugly, an outsider. I hadn't felt hatred from anybody for a long time, and he hated me. He continually tried to shock me, but I was professionally impressed by his efforts. For a class presentation in which I ask the students to prepare a theatrical collage about their own lives, he came unprepared, as usual. He simply related every moment of a weekend in his northern town. I knew he hadn't prepared this "solo" piece, as others had spent a great deal of time preparing, and he thought he was putting something over on me. But what he did was theatre at its best. It was simply brilliant and ready for any professional stage. I just wish he had had a bigger audience.

He resisted Shakespeare, at first, as being part of my world, I suppose, and nothing to do with holding court at bars and backyard swimming pools or drag-racing drunk through the main street of town. One day in class I was helping him with a monologue in which the character declares his hatred for another character; he recited without any affect. I asked him if he had ever hated anybody. Something flared in his eyes and when he did it again he was brilliant. I told him so. A few minutes later I was in the washroom and I heard him walking by with friends: "And when she asked me if I had ever hated anyone I wanted to say, Yeah you, you fucking bitch."

It was hard to believe, but I had an enemy. I suddenly felt that I was in a Shakespearean drama. I felt threatened, but also challenged, in the mode of a Shakespearean character. What I ask myself now is, How did I make my choices in this scenario: as a detached and calm and wise teacher, or as a scared girl, or as a dramatist? Did I know on some level that to ask him, "Have you ever hated anybody" was possibly offensive to him, and therefore dangerous to me?

One day the students were presenting their scenes for 25 per cent of the final grade. This young man and his scene partner were next. I saw him putting on his coat, and asked him where he was going. He said he was going to meet a buddy. I told him that he was obliged to stay and perform his scene, that his partner was prepared, and that out of respect for her he should stay. He stayed, performed well, and then left. I was offended at his leaving so quickly, and gave the class a short lecture on professionalism. From that moment on he was openly hostile. His hostility was so great that I approached him privately one day, and apologized for having offended him. I told him I thought very highly of his work and I hoped we could communicate. He murmured the right things, without any eye contact, and went his way. But the hostility became worse. Apparently I had "centred him out." Oddly, he enrolled in my 300-level acting course the next semester. I was careful around him, and slightly fearful. He had changed the power dynamic. I was a woman, and I was intimidated. One day I was coaching him and another male in a scene from *Othello* in which Iago enrages Othello and we see the full force of Othello's jealous rage—this student's anger was like nothing I had ever seen. He scared the student playing Iago, and he scared me. It was as if there was lightning coursing through his body; his eyes were those of an attacking animal; his voice was like an exploding building. At one point in the scene, he, who had never broken the "fourth wall," looked out at me, the only other person in the room, and said his line: "I will tear her to pieces, I will tear her to pieces." Long pause. And then he resumed the scene with his partner.

He had become the wild animal, just as I had while playing Helen Keller. His scream, like my screams, had transformed him, and sickened the audience. He had done the unthinkable: he had threatened a teacher, exerted power over the oppressor, and made me cower. He had risen from the rank of student and, for a moment, had become king.

A moment of theatre. Did I stop the scene? Did I confront him there and then? I wish I had. No. I did the cowardly thing he knew I would do, because he had a diabolical ability to perceive weakness. I was trying to give him the benefit of the doubt, although in my gut I knew there was something very wrong. And I was probably afraid of him at that point. So I did nothing. But I was up all that night.

The next class, I quietly approached him at the break and said that I wanted to point out that he had broken the fourth wall during the coaching session, and he looked at me boldly and said, "I know exactly what I did." At this moment he had all the power. I was a scared little girl and he was one of the guys who had thrown pennies at me. I think I gave him a nervous smile and said, "Oh good, well at least you know …" and moved on. I did not confront him.

Had he threatened me because he feared a low mark over poor attendance? I didn't even consider that for the longest time, because his work was so strong. He finished the course and he got a good mark, because his acting was brilliant. I still wonder what would have happened if I had given him a poor grade. Or if I had had the courage (or recklessness) to give him a poor grade, if he deserved it. Wouldn't just giving him an "A" be much easier than enduring further threats or even violence? Luckily, I never had to struggle with that question. Even so, as long as I knew he was on campus, I was frightened.

I walked a mile out of my way at lunch every day to avoid him on campus. One day he saw me, and walked with me. "Would you like some help, Judith? You look real discombobulated." His manner was extremely menacing, so I ignored him. I was shaking from my toes to my scalp. Even though I was trying to persuade myself that he intended me no harm, I knew kinetically that he was a danger. My animal instinct to flee overwhelmed me.

Of course, I reported the incidents to the department Chair and others, but when I was at the university I lived in fear. I am still fearful—and yet, I will confess that there is an element of drama in the danger that I find professionally compelling. I ask myself hard questions: Did I make the choices I made in my interaction with this student as a teacher in order to keep everything calm, or as a dramatist looking for the most dramatic outcome? Should I modify my teaching style so that these moments of animal rage remain contained, and restrained? Or was he just a wild card, the enemy we all have waiting for us somewhere?

I am afraid that if I teach in a more conventional way, the genius in each student will no longer be revealed in my class. Instead, the students will remain inside the caul that we all must wear to survive in this world. I think there is peril in all art. In fact, there is no art without peril.

As a teacher, I have finally become the student I should have been in school: I am greedy to learn from each experience, because I know I will be stronger and more able when the next rough and dangerous moment happens. But just as I feel that, I return to a state of innocence, of deafness and blindness and trance each time I write. I must approach every new semester in a state of readiness and child-like innocence, unarmed, but with seeing eyes and enduring respect for the sometimes dangerous power of theatre.

(2003)

"It's My Birthday Forever Now": Urjo Kareda and Me
by Judith Thompson

This essay was written for a special issue of Canadian Theatre Review *honouring the memory of Urjo Kareda, artistic director of Tarragon Theatre from 1982 until his death in late 2001, and a mentor of Judith Thompson and dramaturge for much of her work at Tarragon Theatre.*

I am afraid to write about Urjo Kareda because to write about Urjo is to write about myself: I cannot pretend to be an impartial observer. He was as integral to my development as a playwright as my hands are to my body and as the limestone is to Kingston, the southeastern Ontario town I grew up in. I fear my own narcissism as I write about Urjo, because I can only see the man in terms of my own history: from a raw and reckless young actress/writer sitting in his famous office, overwhelmed by his presence and his breathtaking intellect to a still raw but somewhat more careful, more conscious middle-aged playwright who aches with grief and regret and even petty jealousy every time I conjure his voice or image in my mind.

I will move backwards here, from my personal regret and self-recrimination to the shining "it's my birthday forever now" beginning.

Sitting in my office at the University of Guelph where I teach playwriting, screenwriting and acting, I feel Urjo. I thank Urjo, for without his support, I wouldn't be here, able to learn from my students, to share my practice, my mistakes, my epiphanies with them. And more directly, there is to my right, on my shelf, the last postcard from Urjo, a thank-you note for the large bouquet of flowers I sent him after I learned that his melanoma had spread to his brain and to his lungs. The postcard, which I have enlarged and framed, is of a white, two-story wooden house of the kind one sees in the Maritimes, turned over on its side, almost on its roof, against the backdrop of a blue sky with the barest breath of a white cloud. On the other side is his note: "Dearest Judith—Thank you for the glorious bouquet of flowers—as if from a 'Perfect Pie' landscape … With love from Urjo." Dated "4/12/01."

He died twenty days later. Every day that I walk into my office, I encounter Urjo in his handwriting: smart and stylish; it is like a drug to me; every time I see that hand-writing, I flush, intoxicated with his presence, with the expectation of the brilliant dramaturgy, the flashlight-in-the-dark attention to my work, my deepest self; his astonishing poetry of expression that just left the reader breathless. As many of his friends and colleagues have attested, his letters were poems, electrifying, eloquent expressions of his mind and his heart—praising extravagantly, criticizing incisively, being the zeitgeist, the audience, and the artist and sometimes the kindly spiritual father all at once.

So, although I am momentarily intoxicated by the sight of Urjo's hand, the intoxication is followed by a flash of the horror of his suffering, and the suffering of his family and then, selfishly, my own regrets move in, all the "if onlies": the wishes—I wish, for example, when I look at that postcard, I had never accepted the commission from CanStage to write *Habitat*, my last play. I was a whore, I tell myself. I wanted the money and the big stage. It seems it was ill-fated from the start. I had premiered all my plays since *White Biting Dog* at Tarragon Theatre, under the guidance of Urjo, and when CanStage called, I really couldn't say no. It would be the first time a play of mine had ever been in an "A" theatre with almost a thousand seats. It would be an opportunity to write a play specifically for the big stage, to discover what that might mean. And it was a good thing for Canadian theatre and the money was serious money, critical for a family of seven with massive debts and continuing needs.

I remember meeting Urjo for a delicious, long luncheon of minestrone, salads and gelato at the Faema Café at Christie and Dupont. It was a bright, hot summer's day shortly after my commission was announced. Urjo seemed a little hurt about the commission, somewhat brusque but also happy for me. He was excited about the freedom I would have to write a multi-character play, a large play, and he looked forward to working with me again after *Habitat* was finished. I promised to show him the play as it developed, then we left the subject and had a lively, warm conversation. Urjo and I shared a kind of child-like fascination and almost disbelieving amazement at the miracles and the brutal realities of our lives. We would shake our heads about something unfathomable but utterly real and both murmur, "I know. I know!" When we left each other that day, our friendship was bright as the day, and strong and real.

So what happened? As I got deeper and deeper into *Habitat*, with workshops and then rehearsals which began in August 2001, I became monomaniac, utterly selfish and obsessed with getting the play right. I was working with Iris Turcott, a formidable dramaturg and with the extraordinary company of actors led by Stephen Ouimette and Holly Lewis. After rehearsals, I would race home to my five children and after shopping, cooking, cleaning and helping with homework, refereeing the inevitable sparring between children, I'd prepare for the coming semester at Guelph. I wanted Urjo's guidance; I needed Urjo's guidance but I was too ashamed to give him the play until it was in better shape. I kept putting off the moment and finally, in tech rehearsal, I asked my brilliant colleague Caroline Azar to please give the script to Urjo. She did. But it was too late. He did not respond.

Although Tarragon was thanked in the program, Urjo did not attend the play. When the run was over in October, I faxed him a note:

Dearest Urjo,

I think of you every day. I would love to meet, to talk with you in the next while about my next play, and the one after; of course I would also like to talk about the nightmare experience of you know what— a text I love, actors I love but but BUT. And I want to explain every- thing—about the Excursion—are you free for lunch on any day except a Monday or Wednesday? Next week or the week after?

Love,

I was wagging my tail and bowing my head at the same time, a little bit sheepish and fearful, but excited about working on my next play with the Great One. I will not include his response because it was written only for me, but I will say that he was upset with me. First for giving him the play when he felt it was too late for badly needed input—he was right about that; he was absolutely right. Secondly, he was dismayed that I had written a play that, in fact, was not a multi- character, large play and could have gone into a small space easily and thirdly, for an interview in *Canadian Screenwriter* in which I was incorrectly reported to have said that Iris Turcott was the best dramaturg with whom I had ever worked. I had said, "one of the best," but I do garble my words and speed-talk sometimes and so, Urjo, understandably, felt attacked. He said the play was deeply disappointing and he did not attend because he knew that it couldn't be staged. He said it was not a good time to meet with me because I was still in the world of *Habitat* and we should wait a long time. His letter left me shattered, a frightened and disbelieving child. Not Urjo; he couldn't be angry at me; he has never been angry at me. I sat at my computer all night composing replies—hurt replies, angry replies, clever replies. Finally I just replied, honestly and without any rancour.

Dear Urjo,

Although it is true I am still in the "world of *Habitat*" and it is like my newest child—I love it ardently and protectively—it is, in a way, a very good time to meet with you. Partly because I am readying it for publication, and I would very much welcome your thoughts. (I know it is not perfect.) And I think we need to connect now before a freeze sets in. Don't you? I feel quite desperate about it.

Etc., etc. Jump to the end:

Anyway, I am so sorry that there are any bad feelings. My relationship with you and Tarragon is one of the most important in my life. Me going down there for one show was only ever about the co- commission with MR [Manchester Royal] Exchange [Theatre] and the money, frankly, which I really, really needed for the house and children.

Love,

A day later, I heard the crackle of the fax machine and held my breath as I saw the Tarragon logo. Urjo had written me a brief, conciliatory note, suggesting lunch at the end of the week. I was so relieved.

But then something came up, something stupid like a dentist's appointment and I had to cancel. We agreed on the next Friday. Then on Thursday, 1 November, the fax machine crackled again. Urjo was cancelling our lunch because he had just received news that his cancer had spread to his lungs and they were planning further tests. I wrote a letter to Urjo which I did not send. Instead, I hand-delivered a card to Tarragon.

To my surprise, he was actually at the theatre that day, and I went nervously to his office, but he had stepped out. I put the card on his desk, and wandered around that area of Tarragon for five minutes, and got the ridiculous sensation (borne of childhood abandonment issues, I suppose) that he was hiding from me. Imagine this larger-than-life man hiding in the costume closet, or under his desk. Ridiculous, but I was sure of it, and I absolutely didn't want to intrude on him. So I left. I should have intruded; it would have been the last time I saw Urjo, touched him, hugged him, and may even have received absolution from him. And I was so worried about intruding that I left. It is the stuff of theatre the way our childhood issues can intrude on, and can change the path of our lives.

I take nothing at all for granted anymore. I realized that I had committed the sin of complacency because I sometimes took Urjo's presence in my life and career for granted, as if everything I wrote deserved to be read by Urjo Kareda. I remember grumbling to someone in the business about the critics, and she snapped "at least you get everything you write performed."

I had been very, very lucky.

Right now, Urjo is standing behind me, looking at the screen. I can feel him, slightly breathless, standing over me. I am not sure what he is thinking though. He is just reading right now, and considering.

Now, like most other playwrights, when I write a play, I have absolutely no assurances that it will be performed. I will have to send it around and talk it up, sell it, like an Avon product. Braham Murray, the Artistic Director of the Royal Exchange Theatre in Manchester, England, where *Habitat* was produced in November 2002, said to me "I am very glad you are still writing plays because most playwrights have only a ten-year lifespan." I felt as though I had been slapped into reality. Of course. That is why I have felt a sort of animosity from some of the theatre community, and certainly from some of the critics, as if they feel that my time should be over now. It has been ten years. But Urjo always saw me as the young, raw, struggling playwright that I see myself. Never "established" or "mid-career" or "senior" but always climbing, discovering, uncertain, grateful.

Urjo and I had a polite, empathic relationship; he was fairly paternal with me, which I invited, and yet always respectful. Of course there were a few moments of tension before the final one. Urjo would suddenly bite sometimes and it was always a shock. When we were discussing the production of *Perfect Pie* and I sat in his office telling him how I had decided that I would like to direct the play, he mentioned that he was excited about an idea of mentoring. He had a notion to bring in a young director who would be a sort of protegé and almost co-director. His argument was enticing, and powerful, but when I thought for a moment, I realized it wouldn't work. I did not want to co-direct because I need a direct line to the actors, from my instincts to the stage. The staging of a play, of course, becomes part of the writing. When I haltingly told him of my feelings that I should direct the play on my own, he was offended—he thought I was implying that he was disrespecting me and he spoke to me sharply. I felt as though I had been struck with a knife. I looked at the floor and didn't speak for a full minute. I couldn't imagine myself being a mentor-as-a-director, and so I thought he did not trust my directing ability and wanted someone else as security. He was angry at my misinterpreting him. So there is the stuff of theatre again: serious communication problems as a result of childhood issues.

Urjo had true loyalty to his writers, as long as we showed loyalty to him. We could write freely, abandoning all self-censors, knowing that unless it was just a preposterous, insulting piece of tripe, our work would get produced on the Tarragon stage. He would be there to help us pound it into shape.

His first response to a piece was always a beautiful note—of course I am kicking myself for not having saved any of them…. They were along the lines of "thank you for this harrowing, and exhilarating piece of work. You have touched my very soul. Nan's journey is deeply funny, insightful, and yet a trenchant social criticism, unlike anything you have ever written and I will be a slave of this play until I die." That last sentence is one he actually wrote about *I Am Yours*. It is tattooed in my brain.

Then we would have a meeting in his famous office. Urjo would explain to me his two or three pages of written notes, and I would respond. I almost always agreed with him. Sometimes, I didn't. Usually in hindsight, he was right. In later years, he would often fax me the notes. I would shriek with delight when I read them because he was so on, so there, so right. I felt rescued. I would implement his suggestions as soon as I had read them. He could always see when I had wandered off the path, or I had contradicted myself (which was frequent) or given all the children of one character the same name, or had them wearing coats and scarves in July, or had just really alienated the audience with something particularly disgusting. Although he was very supportive of the idea that "nothing human disgusts me," at the same time, he hated anything that was gratuitously disgusting. He was protective of his audience, but never the shoe-shiner as are so many artistic directors. And always, always, he would ask, "Where are the jokes?" because humour not only delights and connects an audience but in the darkest play, humour is hope. *Sled* didn't have the humour of some of my other plays and

Urjo worried about that. He was correct. The audience, by and large, did not connect with that play; in fact, many of them actively hated it.

I had a difficult moment when, after a disastrous critical reception, I had been approaching a nervous breakdown, crying for days and nights on end when my children were at school or asleep. (I now realize that it was mainly because I was newly pregnant and didn't know it yet.) I was unable to leave the house because of the public shaming of the terrible reviews, and the antipathy of the audience. Urjo and I met for lunch. We talked about one of the critics who was particularly vicious. He looked at me and said he wondered if it were possible that she was in any way accurate. Great big tears dropped into my pumpkin soup. He comforted me. He loved much in the play. But what he was saying was important. We can't fall so deeply in love with our own work that we completely ignore all negative feedback. It's one thing if the audiences are deeply moved and the critics who happen to be writing for the dailies at the time hate it; but if the audiences are as unmoved as the critics, we had better listen up.

Urjo reminded me that we are writing to communicate, and after his death, I learned the hardest lesson of my life on communication. If I had only kept open my communication with him, instead of letting my fear of criticism keep me from showing him *Habitat* earlier. If I had stayed and waited to hand him the card in person, and put all my love and gratitude into a hug, if I had e-mailed him more, bombarded him with love, instead of the two tasteful, short e-mails I did send. Shyness and fear of rejection become failures to communicate.

I can still feel Urjo leaning over me. And I look at him, into his water-blue eyes. He says, "I was so MAD at you. I was really never going to speak to you again. But I can't stay mad at you; you know that. I forgive you, posthumously."

Yes, this is my fantasy. Because until you forgive me, Urjo, I will not forgive myself. I know you are watching me, as you watch so many others, those who are more worthy of your watching than I. I can feel your hand on my shoulder as I write. I can hear your voice and see your eyes looking right through the woman I seem to be to the soul, to the well, the muck, that is where the plays come from. The plays that will always be for you.

Love,

(2003)

Witnessing the Workshop Process of Judith Thompson's *Capture Me*: Mothers, Masks and Monsters:[1] A Conversation Between Teacher and Student

by Robyn Read

I first met Judith Thompson when she was my professor for an Acting Studio course at the University of Guelph. We were performing *Hamlet* and she directed me to reach the core of Ophelia's madness by "standing in the blood" of my character. At her request, I went outside on a muddy spring evening and rolled in the slush until I felt physically agitated and a little uncivilized as students passed by me on their way to the library. I had taken a risk, leaving my safe, known body to inhabit another. When I returned to the stage, proud of my transformation, she informed me that I was still not quite monster enough. "Robyn, you do not have enough shit in your hair," she said, offering me the kindest of smiles, and I went back outside to rummage through the leaves.

Two years later, Thompson offered me the opportunity as a graduate student to assist in the workshop rehearsals for *Capture Me*, her sixth play to premiere at the Tarragon Theatre in Toronto.[2] *Capture Me* is the story of Jerry Joy Lee, (Randi Helmers), a kindergarten teacher who is stalked by her ex-husband Dodge Kingston, (Tom McCamus). Dodge is a former university professor who reforms troubled youth at the local jail by giving seminars on violence. He attempts to rehabilitate children while struggling against his own evil instincts. Jerry has an obsession of her own; after many attempted phone calls where she is unable to speak, she at last makes contact with her biological mother, Dr. Delphine Moth (Nancy Palk). However, the restoration of Jerry's faith, a woman both pursued and abandoned, is a responsibility her mother refuses to accept; it is left in the hands of her friend and fellow teacher Minkle (Chick Reid), and the father of one of her students, Aziz Dawood (Maurice Dean Wint), whom she falls in love with. After witnessing the massacre of his family, save his daughter Sharzia, he has fled his home and does not speak of his past.

In the play, almost every character is a teacher or has been a teacher, and much of the action takes place inside a classroom. Teaching is an institution that Thompson feels saved her life both as a playwright and as a mother by paying her to employ her artistic skills in the classroom ("'I Will Tear You To Pieces'" 27). However, she was not conscious of the prominent role that teachers played in *Capture Me* until after she had finished the first draft. I witnessed how the workshop process functioned like a mirror: what at first seemed to be the story of the Other ultimately reflected a kind of fear that Thompson knew personally.

Near the beginning of the play, Dodge embarrasses Jerry with a particular memory: he reminds her how she used to get up in the middle of the night hungry, go to the fridge and stuff a cold potato in her mouth. The audience shares an emotion with the protagonist that is as simple, yet as heartbreaking, as humiliation; we have all met this monster. Thompson recalls her own shyness, an anticipation of embarrassment that made her dread facing a classroom of students during her early days of teaching. In *Capture Me*, in various ways, teachers philosophize about both what they fear and hate, and act upon their rage.

Dodge preaches, "Every person in this world has become a monster at one time or another, you aren't the only ones" (*Capture* 45). Thompson explores how rage may simmer just below the surface of all people, staging relationships between the victimized and the villainous that reveal both the existence of boundaries and their fluidity; neither monster nor human is an autonomous body. Judith Thompson is teaching her audience to re-invent or perhaps simply re-interpret the monsters in our civilization, with a play that brings those previously on the periphery, historically alienated as Other, to centre stage. *Capture Me* is a play about transformation, transmogrification, and becoming what we most fear.

***

Robyn Read: In the article "'I Will Tear You To Pieces': The Classroom as Theatre," you state the following:

> To write, I have to become, basically, a child who is a wild animal. The rest of the time, I am an ordinary, rather slow-witted but good-humoured woman, the kind of mother who falls asleep in front of CBC documentaries at ten fifteen every night, and does two loads of laundry before waking the kids at eight in the morning. (27)

Before we look at the monsters in *Capture Me*, I'd like to ask you how being a mother has influenced your writing.

Judith Thompson: Let's start by taking a look at children: a wealth of new, profound experience, in which I experience an ecstasy I never thought possible, a grace I never thought possible and a love I never thought possible, and altruism, as well as constant self scrutiny. Any mother will tell you that her greatest fear is that she's not a good enough mother: what did I say wrong? Why were they so angry when I asked them to get their shoes? You know, am I doing the right thing? And I think self scrutiny is really good for a writer, because most of us may walk around half comatose, speaking without thinking, there's so much we do that's un-scrutinized. And good people try to think, or over think, but as a mother, if you're a mother with a conscience, you have to constantly be scrutinizing your behavior. Like, "Mommy, why are you talking in that fake voice to your friend?" You don't get away with anything! Because children love you in your honest more pure state. So as a writer, you have to constantly scrutinize, because things you do are going to cause huge reactions, sometimes without you knowing; you have to ask yourself was that an honest insight, was that an original insight, where am I going there? It's not that it inhibits you; it actually frees you by opening a door to your unconscious by being a mother and responding to yourself and your baby on intuitive levels.

RR: How is this ability to scrutinize, that you've developed as a mother, related to your work in theatre? For example, how is it related to mask work, an activity that is not only a crucial part of your writing but also your pedagogical practice? How do students react to letting their inhibitions go, trying to fight the academic instinct to analyze their work?

JT: It always works great. I'm creating my own play right now with masks, and it's a new frontier for me, or perhaps a return, I'm returning to a moment from twenty-five years ago. The students have to physicalize, they have to connect their body, and once they do something to their body they lose their identity, and once they lose their identity then the id can come out like a waterfall. All the scripting comes out, it's a first draft. The scrutinizing is saved; it is part of the revising, the unperformed self.

RR: In a few articles you have discussed the inspiration for *Capture Me*, which came from the experience of teaching a student who had a history of aggressive behavior that seemed to occasionally surface in the classroom. You saw this student release an unguarded emotion within him. What took place between that initial moment where you witnessed his rage and the writing of the play?

JT: It's never a conscious effort to write about a specific experience. It's a matter of what stays with me, in a way, what sinks in. I remember with my first play, *The Crackwalker*, I was working as an assistant to an adult protective service worker, and a baby died, was killed by a mentally challenged client, and I was the one who answered the phone, and I was horrified, and I wasn't even mature enough to fully grasp the horror. So when I started amusing myself writing these Kingston characters—it was a gross attitude I had in a way, I found it funny, like doing a SCTV routine where I would play with the Kingston accent—but without *my* permission, this story came rushing through. It demanded to be told, it's like automatic writing, but I never made a conscious effort to say, "I am going to write a story about that baby dying," it was Teresa and Sandy, their voices I liked, and what I felt about it, but didn't even really know because I didn't even really know myself yet.

RR: You and I have discussed Susan Brison's book *Aftermath* in the past, a book that explores the remaking of a self after an experience with violence. She states:

> Our deepest fears, joys, and desires are embodied in the chemical signals of our neurotransmitters. We are our own creators of meaning, making up—and made out of—our histories, our idiosyncrasies, our crazy plot-lines, our unpredictable outcomes. (83)

Capture Me is not autobiographical, but it is about a particular kind of fear that most women, at one time or another, have faced or will encounter. How much of the writing process is a reaction to the writer's own make-up or history?

JT: It's a way of healing, too, without even knowing that you're doing it. There was no other way I could deal with what happened. With me the worst didn't happen, but I could feel, without any doubt, with certainty, that given the right situation it would have.

RR: I think it has to do with our instincts that can become quite heightened in situations where we feel something could, or is about, to happen. Maybe we develop these instincts later in life and then after the moment, after the fact, we can use these instincts to instruct how we re-connect to, or re-evaluate, the situation. Did you have to inhabit Dodge in order to understand the type of monster that he could become?

JT: I only inhabited the good part of him. I inhabited him during his talks because I learned a little about Kant and radical evil and I thought, what would I like to say to these boys if I really wanted to help them and help make the world better? Now as far as the other part of him, I've been in states where I've been irrational or unreasonable. You get in an argument with someone, even a friend, and that friend asks you to just stop, you know, let's go for a walk or something, but you're in that mode where you can't stop. It's this weird altered state you get into when arguing, and it's like you have to almost break a spell to get out of it. And I think that's what he's in.

RR: How important was the workshop process to develop Dodge's spells?

JT: Well you have the spells, and you have the lectures. The spell is like when he sees [Jerry], on a road walking, for example, and it's like being on a diet and you haven't had anything sweet for a week and nothing's going to stop you, you've decided, and nothing's going to stop you from having that treat. It's the same with alcohol and alcoholism. That's what Tom [McCamus] and I decided it was. So with Dodge, he vaguely knew if he ever saw Jerry again what might happen. He gets a little job offer, he says yes, kidding himself, and then looks around where she might be living, and as soon as he sees her he's like the skier going down the Alps—that is his historical determination, skiing down that hill. You can't fight the gravity, and you can't fight the hill, you can't ski backwards. He's gender scripted, and his hate for women is overdetermined. We all were struggling for a while, but the workshop for me was a way to articulate these ideas clearly, balance the play, refine and cut the "music" of each scene.

RR: When you have to be in an atmosphere where you are able to listen carefully and think clearly and concentrate, how was the workshop process affected by having two students, Dalbir Singh and myself, present? We were at the rehearsals to assist you, but at the same time you must have been conscious of the fact that we were your students, and we were there to learn.

JT: You know, maybe for only about half a day or even an hour I would have been slightly shy having you there? Because although I talk about my process with my students, as you see, there are aspects of it that could be embarrassing. On the other hand I knew you both well, and trusted you both, and, as you saw, the needs of the play take over. Especially with you both there from the beginning, it wasn't long before I felt totally free.

RR: We've discussed finding a way to provide this opportunity for future graduate students, to assist or at least observe workshop rehearsals [at Tarragon while studying at the University of Guelph]. Do you think this is a worthwhile venture?

JT: Well, yes, but you're the student. Do you think it was worthwhile?

RR: Definitely. For me it was very important to have an opportunity where I got to see my teacher as also a practitioner; I think it's important for any drama student, especially at the graduate level, to see how the teaching and the art work with each other, out in, you know, the real world.

JT: What difference did you notice?

RR: I guess I saw a trust that I don't see in the classroom. In the classroom you have students, and they're respecting you in a sense because you're the teacher, but they don't always trust each other or themselves because they're new to theatre, they're just learning, they aren't experienced yet. What I witnessed with *Capture Me* was an environment with professionals who trusted each other and themselves, and carefully listened to their instincts and your instincts, didn't overanalyze or agonize every step because they knew that you understood rhythm. Most importantly they had faith that that process would eventually work, because they had experienced the process working in the past. They had experienced success on some scale. There's a shyness that happens in the classroom that I think is different from that professional situation.

JT: Is it that the students are shy?

RR: Well, yes, maybe insecure is a better word. They're doing things to overcompensate for their insecurity as students, and it ends up hindering their performance as actors.

JT: Oh, right, so not listening ... that can be pretty annoying, especially when I am used to an atmosphere of mutual trust and exploration together. Also that's why I sometimes resent having to put on a mask of pedagogy or expertise. The best work is work we all stumble through together.

RR: When you and Tom were working on Dodge, did you discover the character together? Many theorists believe that the monster reflects some greater truths about the human condition; the monster is a mirror that reflects aspects of humanity that are both good and bad. What did you discover that Dodge represented or symbolized? For example, in a previous interview you told me that, in a way, Dodge represents Canada, a country that has fought against itself, with a history of violence against First Nations People.

JT: Right. Dodge is like a country trying to fight the forces of destruction within itself, but nevertheless allows them, and that's how it, or he, fails. All these terrible things happen, and we allow it, but the problem is that we don't scrutinize ourselves, and question how did we allow it? How is this happening?

RR: In that sense, Dodge, the monster, is at an opposite pole to the mother because he is not able to scrutinize what he is doing.

JT: That's right, he doesn't look inward. Jerry is trying to make him at the end, telling Dodge that he is a good person; he is a good person inside.

RR: He assumed that Jerry would mother him back to the state of being human. But it seems like he didn't realize that by mothering him she would also have a responsibility to scrutinize, to say look at yourself, look at the parts of yourself you can control. He just wanted her to love him no matter what; he didn't want to have to change.

JT: That's right, he just wanted unconditional love. He thinks that if he can get Jerry, and own her, that he will be human again, somehow.

RR: What about Aziz, where did the inspiration for Aziz come from?

JT: The Other. That we think that's what to be feared is what's invading, the interloper, the Other, when really what's to fear is inside ourselves. Aziz also gives, for Jerry, the perfect heterosexual romance, as opposed to the nightmare she had with Dodge. It's what every woman dreams of: the knight in shining armor that always comes from some far off place because he is not the man you know. On the other hand, he's also representing how we look at immigrants and how we stereotype them. In fact, I think one review said that he was dangerous, something about him being unclear yet clearly dangerous, but he's not dangerous in any way at all. That's a projection of the audience, and that's what I'm interested in.

RR: You say Aziz provides an ideal heterosexual relationship, yet it's not a sexual relationship. Where did that choice come from?

JT: Because the sexuality is secondary. They're meeting as human beings, as souls. And then, if things had gone on, he might have married her and, according to his faith, sexuality probably would have been a part of that. But I think that relationships between the sexes can be corrupted by the primacy of sex, basically.

RR: The absence of the sexual relationship is what made me consider that perhaps Aziz is serving a maternal role.

JT: Yes, I mean, I didn't intend it, but it's true because the maternal role is unconditional love; just as a father loves his daughter for who she is, it's a pure love between a male and a female. With Aziz and Jerry they do long for each other, but he saw through Western decadence which can be about power, about conquering something, which is not about becoming intimate with or getting to know the most vulnerable part of someone. I knew I couldn't have the sexual aspect to Aziz's relationship with Jerry, because I realized it wasn't right, because Dodge's obsession with her has to do with sex, it's all about sex. Of course sex represents so much more, ownership, violence.

RR: So we have this parental role, and the opposite, this monster role. So rather than trying to compare Aziz and Dodge, let's compare Jerry and Dodge. What is the connection between the role that Jerry desires, even fantasizes that her mother Delphine will fill, and the role that Dodge plays as an obsessive lover?

JT: Well if you narrow it down, Dodge has a sense of entitlement to her: you were my student, I seduced you, and you were my wife. Women are seen as possessions, literally have been seen as property, for so long, it's our history. With Jerry, her sense of entitlement, well, I guess it's debatable, about how appropriate it is since Delphine is her biological mother but has not been in her life. She still feels that her mother should, in some way, acknowledge her.

RR: There are many monsters and monstrous effects within *Capture Me*; the monster that comes to Delphine is cancer.

JT: Cancer is a stalker that can't be stopped, and it's an epidemic that's from our abuse of the environment. But on a really basic level, it's your body destroying itself. It's an intrepid and invasive disease.

RR: In *Capture Me* there is a distinct difference between how you handle both what is invasive and what keeps a distance compared to your other plays. Julie Adam has previously referred to the monster in your plays as one that is "hovering around the periphery of civilization" (23). How is the monster in *Capture Me* different? For example, in the last scene of the play, it is the humans who are hovering offstage, behind the scrim, while Dodge, the monster, is onstage.

JT: When we fight the monster, when we go to battle with the monster, all our angels, our human influences, the positive and the good, are sort of there with us; they are our weapons, because we don't stand alone. We can't stand alone against the devil or the monster; I think we have to have help.

RR: Minkle, Jerry's friend who is one of those spectators, begs Jerry to "tear [Dodge's] fucking throat out or die trying" (65). But Jerry doesn't do this, she attempts to save Dodge, she tells him that she loves him, as her friend, and she offers him her hand. The instant she touches the monster, it seals her fate; what is the importance of forgiveness in *Capture Me*?

JT: It's not saying that what he's done is okay, it's saying that he's human. If you force yourself to see the monster within the human, then the theory is [he] becomes human, like in a fairy tale. Like kissing the frog. But the trouble is, that's what we wish could happen, but that's not the immediate reality. Now, we can talk about dead bodies on stage, but this is a redemptive moment, because in a way it's our only hope for the world. If we can all see each other as human.

RR: Dodge questions, "how do you stop it? How do you stop this trans-mogrification?" He does end up becoming a monster, killing his former wife; is the message of *Capture Me* ultimately that the reality is we cannot stop trans-mogrification in our society? Or, do you believe that there is a method that we can prevent humans from turning into, or at least acting like monsters, that our society is not employing?

JT: I think one *has* to believe that there is. For some people, of course, it is too late. But [evil] is a root, as in garden or landscape imagery, it has to be uprooted before it has a chance to grow. It has to end with Jerry dead on the stage because that is the reality now; when she reaches her hand towards him, that's not a reality, almost, that's an ideal, what as a society we are hoping for and yes, what certain religions say we should do, and what the world should do. But then I'm trying to contrast that with what does happen, because that is not the way we behave, and that is how we pay: with dead women.

RR: Has your work on *Capture Me* affected your next choices?

JT: I always write a play that's almost sort of counter to what I've just written. What's scary is I write exactly what I always planned to write. With *Capture Me*, I wanted it to be more abstract, poetic, surreal, in reaction to *Habitat*, which was an issue-based, realistic drama. I wanted to return to my theatrical roots. So for the next one, I'm thinking as apolitically as I can, and I just want to see what happens. I'm making myself perform in the next one. It's terrifying, but it's new, it's the next frontier, now that I'm going to be turning fifty, and I've created these characters by myself in a room with a mirror and a mask. There will be someone else; I don't want it to be a one-woman show. But it's a scary thing, so that's why I have to do it.

(2004)

Notes

1 Some of this material was previously presented as "The Transmogrification of Judith Thompson's *Capture Me*: Witnessing the Deconstruction and Reconstruction of Monsters." Association for Canadian Theatre Research Conference. Winnipeg, 29 May 2004.

2 *Capture Me* ran from December 30 to February 8, 2004. The workshop rehearsals took place in October 2003. The actors' names that are provided are from these performances.

Works Cited

Adam, Julie. "The Implicated Audience: Judith Thompson's Anti-Naturalism in *The Crackwalker*, *White Biting Dog*, *I Am Yours* and *Lion in the Streets*." *Women On the Canadian Stage: The Legacy of Hrotsvit*. Ed. Rita Much. Winnipeg: Blizzard Publishing, 1992. 21-29.

Brison, Susan J. *Aftermath: Violence and the Remaking of a Self*. Princeton: Princeton University Press, 2002.

Thompson, Judith. *Capture Me*. Tarragon Theatre, Toronto, ON. Unpublished Script. 10 January 2004.

———. "'I Will Tear You To Pieces': The Classroom as Theatre." *How Theatre Educates: Convergences and Counterpoints*. Ed. Kathleen Gallagher and David Booth. Toronto: University of Toronto Press, 2003.

Beyond the U.S.A., Beyond the U.K.:
A View from Canada
by Judith Thompson

If you asked a random person on the streets of Toronto or Halifax, Moosejaw or Whitehorse, to name one female Canadian playwright, I guarantee you they would be stumped.

If they were committed theatergoers, they might be able to name Djanet Sears, Joanna Glass, and Judith Thompson; Linda Griffiths, Carole Fréchette, and Florence Gibson; Ann-Marie MacDonald and Sally Clark, Maureen Hunter and very few others.

The theatergoer with a burning passion for Canadian drama would certainly name Sharon Pollock and Carol Bolt, Erika Ritter and Betty Lambert, Betty Jane Wylie, Anne Chislett, and even Mavis Gallant. They might actually know about some of the younger, red-hot playwrights, like Claudia Dey and Kristen Thompson, M.J. Kang, Celia MacBride, and d'bi young.

More politically aware theatergoers would know of First Nations (Native Canadian) playwrights Monique Mojica and Marie Clements, Yvette Nolan and Shirley Cheechoo.

But nobody who is not a serious theater scholar would be able to name more than seven or eight women playwrights. Yet there are hundreds of women in Canada whose stunning plays are being produced in small, out-of-the-way venues all over the world, or once and never again in commercial venues. I know, because I recently edited a book of monologues for women, *She Speaks* (2004). There are over eighty time-stopping monologues in this book, with at least seventy by Canadian women.

I am a Full Professor in the theatre program at the University of Guelph, and one day I asked colleague Ric Knowles, while we were collecting our mail after a grueling curriculum meeting, what he knew about women playwrights before 1970. He said that there were "dozens" of books and articles on the subject, and he would loan me a couple he had lying around the office. I followed him, red-faced with shame at my own ignorance, and gratefully received the two books he pulled out for me.

A quick glance at *Women Pioneers: Canada's Lost Plays* (1979), and I learned about Eliza Lansford Cushing, who wrote *The Fatal Ring* (1840); Sarah Ann

Curzon, who wrote *Laura Secord; or, the Heroine of 1812* (1887) and *The Sweet Girl Graduate* (1882). Another book, Kym Bird's *Redressing the Past: The Politics of Early English-Canadian Women's Drama, 1880-1920* (2004), discussed plays by the feminist firebrand Kate Simpson Hayes: *A Domestic Disturbance* (1892) and *T'Other from Which* (1894).

I am overwhelmed by the courage of these women, in such a thoroughly sexist era, to insist upon their voices being heard and enter into such a male-dominated arena. After all, a play brashly penetrates the consciousness of the audience. I am in awe of these women's energy, considering they undoubtedly had many dependents and few conveniences, and that at the time everything was written in ink—there were no little monks at the ready to make copies, no carbon copies—so multiple copies had to be written out painstakingly by hand.

And then, of course, there was stern societal disapproval to contend with. I would bet that many of these women didn't give an owl's hoot about approval. They were goddesses. Early feminists, these pioneers were absolutely certain of the righteousness of their struggle. They believed their voices needed to be heard and knew that there were women who needed desperately to hear what they had to say.

There is something extraordinarily bold about writing a play and actually allowing it to be produced—having the gall to think that the words we put in characters' mouths should be heard, especially the words we put in the mouths of male characters. To have male actors giving their souls to words written by a woman is a marvel, even today in this supposedly post-feminist, don't-they-have-everything-they-want-now? era.

***

I was born in Montreal in 1954. We lived in Kingston, Ontario, for two years and then moved to Middletown, Connecticut, for the next ten, while my father taught at Wesleyan University. My family returned to Canada in 1967, when Canada was celebrating her one hundredth birthday. I was twelve, so I adapted immediately to my surroundings, developing the Scots-Irish-inflected Southern Ontario accent, mastering the local dialect and attitude within weeks.

I had played Helen Keller for my mother in *The Miracle Worker* at the Wesleyan University Faculty Players, and I knew that I was an actor, that nothing would ever deter me from my destiny. I also loved to read, having read every *Nancy Drew* mystery by the age of nine, and by the summer of '67 I had started seriously on Charles Dickens. But I had no notion that I would write, despite editing a classmate's first notebook-novel during recess. I do remember being exasperated by her choices and clichés, and enjoying directing her revisions.

I soon began a career at the local amateur theater, playing Betty Parris in Arthur Miller's *The Crucible* (1953), and acting in the same mix of classics and British farce that every amateur theatre in North America was doing at that time and, sadly, is still doing. I first encountered a female playwright at that theatre when I was fourteen. It was a dream-like play called *Aria da Capo* by Edna St. Vincent Millay, and I adored the absurdity, the existential horror, and the profoundly female version of the truth. Like a stone in oil, the sensibility of Millay's art dropped into my consciousness and would inflect everything I later wrote.

When I was sixteen I was thrilled to be cast in *The Prime of Miss Jean Brodie* (1966), a play which Jay Presson Allen adapted for the stage from Muriel Spark's hilarious but disturbing novel of the same name. The writing is deeply influenced by Freudian psychology, which I was to devour in my twenties. I threw myself into Sandy, the homely but passionate observer, the spy, the future writer, the "assassin."

Clearly, this role planted seeds deep inside me. But at the time, the thought of being the aloof observer, never living in the moment, was anathema. I was an actor, and I found playing the role, with its emotional hills and valleys, and intellectual challenges, gratifying. I loved escaping my own life and walking onto the stage, into the frightening and complex world of Miss Brodie and her acolyte-turned-enemy, Sandy. It was, in a way, a metaphor for my own emergence as a feminist and writer: I was in the slow process of throwing off the mantles of the Catholic Church, and the misogynist society in which I had been living. I was coming to understand that being a girl was largely a performance in a play written for us by men.

My first encounter with a play written by a Canadian woman began as a long, crazy poem called *Dr. Umlaut's Earthly Kingdom* (1974), by the Toronto writer Phyllis Gotlieb. When I was seventeen and in the twelfth grade, a drama educator and true mentor, Nancy Helwig, introduced me to Gotlieb's wild-and-woolly rhyming poem about a mad autocrat, and adapted it for the stage. It was an exciting, non-traditional piece of theatre, and I saw that the traditional well-made-play was not the only option.

It was very exciting to be working on the voice of a Canadian woman. All the plays performed in my local high school had been written by men, none of them Canadian. At that time, in the '60s and early '70s, much of Canadian culture was still borrowed; the great tidal wave of nationalism was beginning politically, but was still at a distance culturally. It never occurred to me that our stories, perhaps even *my* stories, would be worth listening to.

My family spent 1972, my father's sabbatical year, in Brisbane, Australia, where I immediately joined a theatre company and began performing the same mix of classics and commercial hits I was accustomed to.

But here was a much more progressive, politically minded group of young people, and they were doing new Australian work, which I couldn't even audition for because of my accent. The plays were electrifying and caused an earthquake inside my growing consciousness. Yes, I thought, we can tell our own stories. We are not appendages of Britain or cultural appendages of the United States. We are not appendages of men. Our voices have been strangled for thousands of years, but it is possible to remove the hand of imperialism and sexism from our throats and sing out.

I returned to Canada and did a degree in drama at Queen's University in Kingston, where the only Canadian plays I encountered were Herschel Hardin's tragedy of Inuit life, *Esker Mike & His Wife, Agiluk* (1971); a drama by Robertson Davies; and a play by a fellow student.

Then Keith Johnstone, the improvisation guru from Britain, came to teach and he turned all my ideas about theatre upside down. He taught that the canon, or what we had been taught was great, might be garbage, and that what the world considered garbage could be great. The least successful person in his class was the most successful. The stars became the outsiders. I didn't know it then, but Johnstone's political approach would have a profound effect on my work. But despite my Australian epiphany, at that time I was still in a firmly colonial mindset. I believed that the "real" theatre was in New York or London. The "real" literature was written by people we didn't know living in "real" cultural centres.

After graduation, I auditioned for the acting program at the National Theatre School and was admitted. I was fulfilling my destiny: I was an actor. But except for Martha Henry, who came in briefly, all our acting teachers were men—most of them, with the notable exceptions of Carl Hare and Pierre LeFevre, were patriarchal, self-serving, lecherous, anti-artistic men.

Pierre LeFevre especially was an artist and teacher in the purest sense of the words. He was a master mask teacher. He brought his box of simple masks into the studio and changed my life. As soon as I put on a mask, a character would not just start forming, but foaming at the mouth. Another's personal history would move into my body, and my own identity would disappear. Yet I had never felt more present and alive. My unconscious life clearly poured into the mask.

Lefevre asked each of us to find a monologue that suited our mask, and I began with a thin monologue by the American dramatist Jules Feiffer (at this point I still would not have thought about finding a Canadian monologue). The piece was amorphous, but the character was well defined: an over-privileged gossip with a distinct and overbearing persona. Soon, however, I began improvising my own monologues, and my performances of these elicited a response that was both shocking and exhilarating: I had found my path in the world.

I still didn't know I was a playwright. In fact the school's director, an American ex-patriot named Joel Miller, told me in my annual critique that, although I had had some success with these monologues, I must not *ever* think of myself as a playwright. I quickly concurred: "Oh, no, Mr. Miller. Me? Write? What would I have to say?"

***

I am glad this happened, as it is a perfect example of the silencing of women, in this case by a man who was an avowed feminist. Years later I had the opportunity, at the opening of my play *The Crackwalker* (1980), to remind Joel Miller of what he had said. The blood drained from his face, and he turned away, for once at a loss for words.

However, men have not always been my silencers. The actor and director Michael Mawson supported me fully and suggested that I find the work of the great American monologist Ruth Draper. Day after day, I went to the library and listened to recordings of her extraordinary art, to her channeling of people from all walks of life, especially the silenced, the disadvantaged, and the oppressed. She shaped their stories into unforgettable monologues that were chronicles of real people, oral histories of distinct and disappearing cultures.

***

The first time I actually sat down and wrote was one very lonely weekend in Montreal. My roommate was out of town, I had neglected to make any plans, and everyone was busy. I felt a loneliness more intense than I have ever felt before or since. Family and close friends were three hours away in Kingston. With crushing and pathetic self-pity, I reflected that nobody cared whether I got up in the morning or stayed in bed, ate or starved.

I now realize that the reason I felt so empty was because, until then, I had only existed in the gazes of the people around me. If they were looking at me, talking to me, criticizing me, I was alive, I existed. Now that there was no one at all with me, I felt as though I did not exist. It was as if the act of writing kept me from disappearing off the page entirely. I existed so long as I was writing.

My roommate's typewriter was sitting there, beckoning, ready for me on the kitchen table. I wandered over and I began writing Theresa, one of my mask characters. I thought it would be fun for her to have a friend, and in walked Sandy. I had no plan whatsoever. I then thought there should be a couple of men in the picture, and I created Alan and Joe. The horror is that the play emerged without warning. The play literally fell out of me, with past experience finding its place, and the silenced finding their voices through me. *The Crackwalker* is still produced constantly around the world, in many languages. I marvel at the simplicity of the creation of this first play. It has never again been so simple.

I gave the play to Michael Mawson, who gave it in turn to Clarke Rogers of Theatre Passe Muraille, which agreed to produce it. I will never forget the first reading in 1979, with professional actors: it was Christmas morning times ten. I was honoured and floored and yet not floored enough to be cowed. I had plenty of notes for the poor actors.

The play was produced in a fifty-seat theatre, and then produced in a large theatre in Montreal. Due to its frank and explicit revelations about four extremely disadvantaged people in small-town Ontario, there were a few hate-filled reviews.

But there were also full-out raves in esteemed magazines and newspapers. Some thought the play an evil walk through the sewers, some called it a masterpiece. The audience responded very strongly, and the buzz grew louder and louder, and the play became part of Canadian theatre history.

After that first play was produced, I became eligible for Canada Council grants. In those days, I could easily live for a year on the twelve thousand dollars a grant awarded, and I wrote my next play, *White Biting Dog* (1984), which was produced by Urjo Kareda at the Tarragon Theatre in Toronto. So began a twenty-year artistic collaboration that would include *I Am Yours* (1987), *Lion in the Streets* (1990), *Sled* (1997), and *Perfect Pie* (2000). Urjo supported me through challenging work, and I owe much of my success to him.

I do venture out of the theatre occasionally. I have written countless radio plays, a few television movies of the week, including "Life with Billy" (1994). I have written two feature films: "Lost and Delirious" (2001), which sold to twenty-three countries and has a cult following; and "Perfect Pie" (2002), which was beset by conflict, but in the end is quite a good film. I enjoy writing for film, but the theatre is my passion, and I will never stop writing for it.

Currently I am creating a new piece by improvising with masks; the working title is *The Secret Creed*. Now that I am fifty, I am inspired to return to my beginnings.

***

A while ago, a German graduate student who was doing her thesis on Canadian Theatre interviewed me in a local Italian coffee house. As I ate spoonfuls of foamed milk, she told me that other Canadian theatre practitioners had told her I had "paved the way" for women playwrights. I regret that I became a little icy at that moment, for I found this offensive. I imagined it on my tombstone: "She Paved the Way." It makes me sound so workaday, dependable— and it just ain't true. The way is not paved for women. The way is thorny, steep, and treacherous.

A casual look at the upcoming theatre seasons across Canada reveals that at least eighty percent of the plays being presented are by men, and in theatres that seat eight hundred or more, eighty percent are by American or British playwrights. A glance at the Toronto Theatre Awards, the Dora's, and you see that nominees for best play have always been overwhelmingly plays by men. The juries might respond that their choices were governed by the reality that most of the plays presented were by men. And so we must look to the artistic directors, who are also overwhelmingly men.

There is one answer: Youth. Young women of all backgrounds must be sought out and encouraged to write for the theatre. We "veterans" must give our time and energy to support them, and the theatre audiences and critics must make a commitment to their work.

Nightwood Theatre, the first visible feminist theatre in Toronto, was founded in 1979 by Kim Renders, Mary Vingoe, Cynthia Grant, and Maureen White, and it developed Ann-Marie MacDonald's megahit *Good Night Desdemona (Good Morning Juliet)* (1990), as well as Djanet Sears' *Harlem Duet* (1997) and *The Adventures of a Black Girl in Search of God* (2002). The theatre runs a development program for women playwrights who are starting out. Called "Write from the Hip," the group meets once a week, and playwrights, directors, and producers are brought in to talk with the women and listen to their work. I met with the group recently in the beautiful, historic Distillery District. There was a thunderstorm during our meeting, and after the readings, when the storm was over, the sunset glowing through the clouds left us all breathless and bonded, glad that we were playwrights, and with an unspoken agreement that we will never stop writing, that we will not be silent.

(2006)

Works Cited

Bird, Kym. *Redressing the Past: The Politics of Early English-Canadian Women's Drama, 1880-1920.* Montreal: McGill-Queen's UP, 2004.

Thompson, Judith, ed. *She Speaks: Monologues for Women.* Toronto: Playwrights Canada, 2004.

Wagner, Anton, ed. *Canada's Lost Plays, vol. 2: Women Pioneers.* Toronto: CTR, 1979.

Hedda & Lynndie & Jabber & Ciel:
An Interview with Judith Thompson[1]

by Ann Holloway

This interview was conducted November 1, 2005 at Judith Thompson's home in the Annex neighborhood in Toronto.

Ann Holloway: When we were doing *Hedda Gabler*, way back when…

Judith Thompson: 1991, I think it was…

AH: 1991.[2] We were mere children at the time, you mentioned that I would make a great Hedda Gabler and I felt very doubtful of that because of my size, because of being heavy, and I now realize having seen Yanna [McIntosh], that an unconventional physicality is actually great for that character.[3] Her body suggested that she didn't belong.

JT: Her arms were very muscular for instance, and mostly women of that period had absolutely no muscles. But, of course, Hedda Gabler rides a horse.

AH: Yes, and she looked very much like she belonged on a horse as opposed to sitting in a parlour.

JT: In a way, like a caged animal, say a tiger, retains all its muscularity and almost the full strength of a wild tiger, just the way it paces in its cage, 'cause it uses every muscle, I think that's really good for Hedda.

AH: Why?

JT: Because she is a caged tiger. That's what she is. Even though she doesn't have an opportunity anymore to ride a horse, and to run in the fields, or to do labour because she's an aristocrat, she's got that incredible physical power—and part of her whole problem is repressing physical desire, so it goes with that caged tiger theme.

AH: I very much got her torment from Yanna's brilliant performance.

JT: Yes, and that was a stroke of genius I think on Ross [Manson]'s part, casting her. Not only is she a brilliant actress, but her being African-Canadian suggests all sorts of things—oppression, repression, having to fight back, a rich interior life that's not always revealed, our own history of racism in our country. It makes it much bigger. I think Ross was interested in the politics of Lövborg's thesis, and I think his casting Yanna was part of that.

AH: And what about the thesis, do you remember?

JT: There's a phrase that Lövborg keeps using…that if we continue on the path that we are on now (and it's funny that Ibsen doesn't mention slavery) the world would self-destruct. That was Ross's concern, so he asked me to play that up in the writing, and I did. I think the casting of Yanna is part of that, because, looking at our history, our country is founded on the genocide of First Nations people, and the racism continues. It's funny, we become her, though. We start to identify with Hedda, instead of "that's that evil other monster." Because so often she's just that awful spoiled woman, and that's what it becomes about. But upon a really close reading I found what Ibsen didn't know, but might have guessed, that she was abused by her father—you can't make this explicit, because then it becomes an issue piece and you don't want to do that, but I know it's there because of her conflict around Lövborg. What made her almost kill him that day on the couch? With her father snoring in the next room, she said "you violated my most personal, sacred…something," which means, I don't know, he put his hand up her skirt. I don't think it meant that he raped her, I don't think so, but I think it meant that he committed what in those days was a violation—but to kill him for that?! He said, "you should have killed me then," and she sort of says "yes, I should have," and then she gives him the gun and makes him kill himself. And I feel what she's doing is taking revenge on her father. Lövborg is a person she feels real desire for, so she hates herself for that, and hates *him* for that. And that's why she married Tesman, because she likes him and respects him, and doesn't feel any passion for him. So they could have their three kids or whatever, be done with it, and he'd be a companion.

AH: Any passionate sexual love would result…

JT: …in hatred…

AH: …self-hatred…

JT: …yes, because it goes back to her father and her father's violation. So it results in this conflict, I think it's interior. I remember I looked into the fact that there was a great suffragette movement in Norway at the time, there were plenty of opportunities for her. And Tesman was certainly…he's not like Torvald in *Doll's House*, he's quite gentle and open to her doing whatever she wanted really.

AH: So she didn't *have* to marry Tesman?

JT: No, no.

AH: Not to keep her reputation or anything?

JT: She says "Tesman is safe and I married Tesman because he's respectable and my father would have approved." But I read the subtext as being that he was safe for her. You know how she says "sometimes I say these terrible things," and how rude she is to Juliana…

AH: …yes, with the hat….

JT: With the hat. And she says "before I have the remorse, I have this feeling of exquisite pleasure." To me that's speaking about the sexual abuse and that horrible guilt of people if the body feels pleasure at the same time they're being violated. That horrible conflict, so that when you get those tingly feelings, it means violation. So, I think he was exploring something enormous and was so far ahead of his time, but, I think, like Freud, a bit of an innocent. The story is that Freud couldn't believe all these Viennese women saying that their fathers were having sex with them. So he said, well, it must be their fantasy, they must have an unconscious oedipal longing. It took Jeffrey Masson years later to say no, these fine Viennese doctors were raping their daughters, it wasn't longing.

AH: To think that it would be more than a few isolated incidents is unthinkable.

JT: It is. And the same to us with child pornography. It's just unthinkable that there could be such a freak, such an evil freak. And yet, apparently, it's all over the internet, and the police say it's just overwhelming. So, I think, and I don't know how much Ross and Yanna agreed with me, but this is something I think is really interesting about the play. Ross's interest was far more the political, my interest as a woman, as a feminist, and as a writer, because I see it in the writing, I see it clearly, is that nothing's changed. And that's why I think the choice to have it contemporary was interesting—still the abuse goes on even though it's more out there and you can talk to people a little more, yet the battle goes on. Hedda wouldn't commit suicide today, that's what I feel. Even though many people who liked the show didn't like the second half as much. I've heard this quite a bit. And I didn't myself, I think it would be better just placed all in one period, it's smoother. The first hour and twenty minutes was just perfect I thought. The second was fine, but just didn't quite match up to the first. It was a bit awkward seeing it in the present with cell phones.

AH: Something was lost that you can't quite put your finger on. You're being taken along, and taken along, and so magnificently, it was such a terrific retelling of that story, and so relevant. But there is something about that modern setting that throws us off, and I'm not really sure why.

JT: Yeah, it's hard to put my finger on. If I had to do it again, or publish it, I would place it all in 1905, right before the First World War. And I did revise everything, people thought that I did much more in the second half but, actually I didn't. I just made it contemporary. I did as much adaptation in the first half as I did in the second half but, it was adapting it to 1905 instead.

AH: I also thought Yanna was hilarious!

JT: Very funny.

AH: I remember in the production that we did at the Shaw Festival that my character was really the only funny thing in it.

JT: That's where I got all the laughs. Bertha, that's right *(laughing)*. Bertha wasn't as funny this time partly because of her accent. Because it's the rhythms that make something funny. She was amusing and gave a wonderful performance, but Ross liked that idea because especially for the contemporary it works—so many people who are immigrants have to take jobs like housekeeping and be treated badly by someone like that.

AH: Perhaps it's because Hedda in this production was so funny that it kind of…

JT: Yes, that's true.

AH: …you don't have those isolated moments of comic relief.

JT: And I pushed that in the writing too. I wanted to make her funnier and wittier. Because in the Ibsen—it's deliberate and I respect it—she's very spare. The way she speaks is very simple and spare and I wanted to give her more lusciousness and more wit. Just to be a bit outrageous. And Yanna took that and ran with it.

AH: And what does that do for the character?

JT: It just makes her harder to dismiss. She's more of a complex person, with more of an interior life, that you can't just say, "oh she's a spoiled bourgeois brat who doesn't like to be suffocated by doilies and wants her parlour." She says "I have my parlour, I must have my salon." See, that's Ibsen trying to solve his problem that he couldn't figure her out so, he himself, I feel, in the second or third draft would see (and I read all his early notes on his drafts) it must be that she wanted this life, like a beautiful Gertrude Stein with artists and famous people in the parlour, that must be it! No, that's not it. But he couldn't figure it out. And that makes it a better play in a way, that he didn't quite know what it was. Because the world didn't know. And even now people don't know. Why does somebody go into rages if you bump into them at the grocery store or have nine items in the line for one to eight? You know I had a woman flip out at me the other day over the fact that I had nine items, and I said "I'm sorry, I'll take it back," and she kept going. And I thought, "well, there's something else going on here."

AH: Yes, yes, that was very clear in Yanna's performance.

JT: Good!

AH: You are literally thinking that. Why is she just flipping out over something as trivial as Julianna's hat?

JT: And she doesn't know why herself.

AH: I wanted to talk a little bit about the sexuality. I remember when we were doing *Hedda* at the Shaw, there was quite an argument about what should go on on that couch when Lövborg finally does come in and they're alone together. There was a big argument with Jim [Mezon, playing Lövborg] and Fiona [Reid, playing Hedda], who firmly believed there was no way they would even touch.

I don't think they wanted touching at all. Or maybe a brush of the hand. And you wanted more.

JT: I wanted more.

AH: And this time you got it *(laughing)*.

JT: This time I got it and I wanted even more than that. And Ross would have gone along with it, but you have to be delicate, they're finding moments and I respect that. You know what I wanted, and I actually think that it would have worked beautifully: I wanted him to take off one of her stockings and for him just to touch her foot and for her to have an orgasm from her foot being touched, because I think of the level of repression that she had, and to see her naked foot! And if they'd just taken the time, they could have. Or her put her stocking in his pocket and she put her boot on so you wouldn't see. And he'd have her stocking. You know I've heard of that, someone having an orgasm from their hand being held because they're so repressed, so ready.

AH: Yes, that could be an incredibly erotic thing.

JT: Wouldn't it be an amazing moment? But they went farther at least. He had his hand up her skirt and his head in her lap. Bergman had them, I'm told, do the whole thing, practically.

AH: Really?

JT: His production where everything was red. But you don't need it all to happen because the point is that it's volcanic. Or it's like the dyke, you take the finger out of the dyke and you see this incredible—human beings.

AH: A brush of the hand was not quite going to accomplish that. This version was much longer than the Shaw Festival version. What do you think you cut out of the first one that maybe you shouldn't have?

JT: Breathing space. I think I was so worried because the couple that I'd seen— Glenda Jackson's for example—were so tedious, that I was sort of reacting against that. I wanted to get to its essence. But I think that I did cut out important breathing space, because after all it's two days and a woman kills herself at the end. So, I found that I needed that time, it needs that time, the actors need that time. I did put in the dance and things, and that was helpful, but I think more. More. It's got to be a really full meal. Because a woman goes from having no plans to kill herself to ending her life. And pregnant. Her pregnancy too, I played this up more in this one.

AH: And the very, very painful knowledge that she's not in love with the man who has impregnated her and must be incredibly conflicted about it.

JT: I think she knows that she would be a horrible mother. And she'd be abusive, not like her father, but as far as pure neglect. She wouldn't be able to love her child and that her child would be in the torment she's in, for different reasons, but the same self-hatred.

AH: Speaking of which, let's move on to *Lynndie England*.

JT: Yes. *My Pyramids or How I Got Fired From The Dairy Queen and Ended Up at Abu Ghraib.*[4]

AH: The Dairy Queen…I know it's factual, but it's just unbelievable how the Dairy Queen advertising dovetails with all the war propaganda. The Jodies and the songs that the soldiers sing, the insidious rhymes that they chant juxtaposed with…

JT: …oh I hadn't even thought of that, Ann…

AH: —really, oh, it's so striking—and it all comes to a head with "brownie explosion." It's one of those gifts, of course, that you picked up on unconsciously. All the names of the ice cream and the slogans…

JT: …the names, you're right…

AH: …that's all propaganda. It's all designed to make us want to eat sugar, which kills. It's symbolic of the whole American culture.

JT: That's why I chose it. I thought, "that's American culture."

AH: It's also an amazing gift from her factual life. First the Dairy Queen and then we're in Abu Ghraib, and they're singing these macabre songs and rhymes. In my mind it's the same thing.

JT: Sure it is. Children's ads for Cheerios, it's all the same thing.

AH: We'll sacrifice our children's health, let them die from obesity, diabetes, whatever. It's all geared to sell, sell, sell. It's all the capitalist system.

JT: That's selling war.

AH: But "brownie explosion"—I just went, "Judy, good one!" And then you do take that over there.

JT: Actually for her revenge moment—that's right.

AH: Explode all those brown skinned people—they're nothing, nothing to her.

JT: Wow, that's good reading that you've done.

AH: Tell me a bit about how this monologue came about.

JT: Actually, originally, I wrote it for a one night, one-off, political cabaret. I thought, great, because I would never write anything from the headlines for fear of being sued. So, I thought, "what a fun opportunity," and that picture of her pointing her thumb at the naked Iraqi prisoners was just so haunting and chilling. I felt as much animosity towards her as anybody, until I googled her and there were 66,000 sites on her. And I thought, "oh, this is interesting, people really care about the situation," and then the first site said (*she speaks in a small town accent*) "are you looking forward to the pictures of Lynndie England gettin' screwed?" Just grotesque. The answers though, I put them directly into the script. I edited them a bit, but I put the most disgusting ones in—the most sexually violent, pornographic, misogynistic things I've ever seen in my whole life. You know—cut off her head, fuck her neck hole…

AH: …fuck her neck hole!!!

JT: Yes, why does sexual desire become hatred and violence? "Why?" it said. "Because she's the skankiest, homeliest bitch we've ever seen." It was all about her being "ugly." Their obsession was with her being a plain woman. And they hated her for that. I don't think a single one mentioned the prisoners, and the injustice, and her obviously acting out the will of the Pentagon and the will of America. No, not at all. There were a select group who would say "oh the ignorant, pathetic white trash in charge of these men"—more people cared about it at that level. It was nothing sexual or about the way she looks. What intrigued me was the sexuality of the reaction and I thought—this is America. This is why sexuality has become so contaminated, it has become pornography, it has become a currency. Desire equals hatred. So, that really inspired me seeing that, and I thought, I really have to go there. It's a big question for me so I have to go there.

AH: And then this whole thing of pushing the ice cream, pushing the junk food, pushing all this stuff that's going to make women ugly…

JT: …and disable them…

AH: …but all women must be absolutely beautiful and perfect.

JT: I was really vindicated because what I found out in the trial, and it's what I guessed, is that she was so enthralled with Charley, her boyfriend there, and so flattered that he paid her any attention, because she didn't get much attention from men, and the attention she got was just a quickie behind the…

AH: …club house.

JT: Exactly. She said, "we didn't do nothing to those prisoners that hadn't been done to me at the club house and those guys are still my friends." And I thought, "yes." It's because it's how women are treated, especially women who are not considered pretty, who are grateful for any attention and aren't going to go tell anybody. She says "at least I'm busy on a Saturday night," so she's deceiving herself into thinking it's a date—and they're all laughing.

AH: I can't help it, I just find that funny. "I used to be the highschool queen, now I got my M-16"—it's ludicrous.

JT: It is funny. Self-deception is funny and sad.

AH: Why do you think that is?

JT: I think self-delusion is funny, and the way she talks is funny. And I do think that unfortunately there is an element of class condescension—that we are laughing, I guess, at her lack of education. We are. That's there.

AH: Lack of status. I find the whole thing absurd finally, going from being fired from the Dairy Queen…

JT: …to then being in charge of 10,000 men.

AH: I did make the assumption that she was a complete loser, but she's absolutely fine material for the war and a perfect target, someone who's got nothing to lose.

JT: She needs the attention of the guys around her. She needs their approval too because it's hell for women in the military. Apparently they're constantly abused, assaulted, mocked, ostracized, and she had to prove to the guys that she was every bit as badass and tough as they were. That's what it was all about, getting into the club. That's why I made the line from the clubhouse to that, because it's all the same, nothing's changed. And the soldiers were getting off on torturing these Iraqi guys and she was just part of it. That's also what's funny, just taking the dog for a walk—it's horrifying, they put a leash on these men, around their necks, and then she turns it into a "Saturday Night Live" skit.

AH: That connection, ugly women are dogs.

JT: Exactly, it's channeling back to all the guys who called her dog and barked. She says, you gonna call me dog? Because one of them, she says, spoke English and said hey, you're a dog. "You call me a dog?!" So all her rage at all the white guys in West Virginia who'd called her a dog or barked, goes against these Iraqi men cause she's now in full power.

AH: And can do anything. Sit and watch the guy eat his shit.

JT: Oh that, that's right. And she's laughing about it. And that's something Waneta [Storms, playing Lynndie] had a bit of trouble with, that moment, because that's a really difficult acting moment. 'Cause what I wanted, what works the best— she did it the first time—is that when you tell that story—she says "so you know he says to the guy, hey wise guy, Iman, uh, fuck him in the butt now." And he says, "I will not do this for your entertainment." And then Ray, he had to take a shit, right, so he takes a shit and the other guy picks it up and says eat his shit and then kiss him." And what she's supposed to do is laugh just like a child laughing, right. But, as an actor, if you don't get on the track, if you're more of an adult, you go oh (*groans of repulsion*), and then he kissed him, "ohhh." That's not as good, though, as just laughter (*high-pitched hysterical laugh*), like a kid, like it's so funny. See, that's more frightening.

AH: And more real.

JT: Because it's just like us laughing.

AH: They're back at the club house.

JT: Yes, just wonderful clean laughter about the most horrible thing.

AH: And that is the thing that binds a group together.

JT: Exactly!

AH: Common laughter at someone lower.

JT: Nothing unifies like hatred and laughter, and those combined—derisive laughter—it's more of a high. She says "whoa, I never got laughs before." So, that was a big high for her. She had an identity.

AH: Laughter is such a source of power, especially for women who are not supposed to be funny.

JT: That's right. Like the funny guy always has a girlfriend who is not funny. I remember that from high school. That guy who you thought would have a funny girlfriend—she would never have a sense of humour.

AH: It's threatening because there's this association—if a woman can make people laugh she's a slut, which implies that she is in charge of her own sexuality, has her own sex drive independent of men.

JT: It's also male-ish. It's competition in a way, because it's penetrative to make people laugh. You're penetrating into their consciousness and you're making a reaction happen. So it's not feminine. Like writing, it's not perceived as feminine because you're penetrating into the audience. You have insights that make them laugh.

AH: A woman owning her humour is the same as owning her sexuality in the eyes of men—one thing suggests the other. So, by making them laugh, she's able to be attractive in her mind.

JT: And gazed upon, people are paying attention. Not the attention of the predatory gaze but, the gaze of the recipient, of waiting, and usually women wait for the man. Also it means that you have an identity that's not given to you, that you've created, and that's not feminine. What's perceived as feminine is an identity that's passive, that's assigned to you.

AH: Do you think that Lynndie's a monster? Do you think there was something psychologically wrong with her?

JT: No, no, no. Absolutely typical. She's a symptom of Western society. Actually, a symptom of almost every patriarchal society, frankly. I won't say it's just Western corruption.

AH: But capitalism has a lot to do with it. That's the whole Dairy Queen connection.

JT: Yes, currency, and looks are currency. She's as responsible as any grunt Nazi soldier, or American soldier, or anybody, in that when we have advantages and the resources of education, affluence and intellect, maybe you or I could step out and say, as very few did—but a couple did—that this isn't right and I'm stepping out and I'm reporting this. That's the Jodies thing, it's very easy to brainwash anybody except people who are psychic superheroes. I think it takes superhuman psychological strength to withstand that kind of brainwashing. Who knows where any of us would be.

AH: Because we all have a desperate need to feel that we belong.

JT: We've all been captive, by love for instance in our adolescence, where you're obsessed with that person and you're not yourself and you give up and compromise yourself in so many ways—it's no different. It's no different. But, yeah, people still detest her. She's just a product—a product of American society. And it's too bad but *much* worse is happening at Guantanamo Bay, that's what she says. She says, "you think me laughing at their willies was bad?"

AH: And that laughing at their willies is so central to the whole fear of women being funny. Because, of course, if you let a woman up on the stage making jokes…

JT: …jokes about your funny little sausage… That's why that picture really got to them. The naked man and her pointing.

AH: Let's move on to *Enoch Arden*.[5] How did you come across the poem?

JT: Tennyson wrote this poem called "Enoch Arden," this epic poem that was groundbreaking at the time, because it was the first time a member of the proletariat had been the protagonist in a long poem; it was usually always nobility, or the struggle of nobility. This was the rough hewn sailor's lad Enoch Arden. And Strauss wrote—I'm not sure if he wrote it after or while Tennyson was alive—but he wrote a score to accompany the poem, for master thespians to travel throughout Europe and perform this great poem with an accompanist playing the music. You know *(singing)* "long lines of cliffs breaking and the beautiful Annie Lee." You've heard the kind of thing, right? And it's still done in chamber series occasionally. It's lovely, but it's really a snore—people are asleep within 10 minutes. So my friend Maria Lamont—remember she was in the revival of *White Biting Dog*, in 1990?—she was struggling as an actress, so she went back to U of T and trained as an opera director. She called me up and said, "look, I have this poem, I think I can get a little workshop money, would you be interested in hearing it and any ideas at all you had about possibly adapting it in some way for the stage?" I thought, "what am I going to do with this dreary, overblown work?" Yeah, I could appreciate there were some beautiful images, but it was really dreary. So, I came up with this idea for Jabber—for this crazy homeless guy. I'm very interested in how we claim narrative as our own. And in fact when we connect to a play, a film, a story it's because it becomes our story, it's a kind of psychic medicine. And so Jabber claims this story from a dusty old volume I imagine he found somewhere in the back of the halfway house and he thought, "that's my life, he's stolen my life!" That's why he says, "well, I met Tennyson and I told him my story and he barreled it back" *(laughs)*—it's one of my favourite lines—"and Tennyson got credit for it." I was just so thrilled to find Jabber and I would just basically sit with the poem open and write as Jabber and it just all came out.

AH: I have to say, the modern vernacular of the Parkdale halfway house scene, whatever you want to call it, is seamlessly interwoven with the actual poetry.

JT: It really works—oddly. That's because he believes it's his story.

AH: It is his story—a man stranded on a desert island. He says "we are so alone in our so called madness, we are like Enoch Arden stranded 10 years on a desert island and nobody sees who we really are, the shimmering souls that we really are."

JT: I'm so glad you chose that one cause that's just my favourite moment.

AH: It plays to the heart of the whole thing to me, and that's the connection that makes it work so magnificently. These people that we've decided to banish to the margins: Jabber says, "that's how people see me out on Queen Street, asking for money for a bus ticket, the solitary gutter rat, hardly human." And they might as well be on Mars. We'd like them to be. Exiled to aloneness.

JT: Incredible aloneness. When you see them and they've slept all night in the park or on the sidewalk—alone. That really was a miracle connection, it just came. The best things just flow through because they need to. And it worked quite well, but then we'd come to rehearsal and there was something really missing. The accompanists we had were fine accompanists but they weren't actors.

AH: So you didn't have the character of Ciel yet?

JT: I had her, I put her in, but Jabber would really just kind of look over at her because she wasn't an actor. And one day I said to Maria—I want Ciel to get up and interact with him—it must be about the two of them. Finally, we had the miracle of getting Kristin Mueller, who, although she was not trained as an actor, is a natural. And when I asked her to get up and go to him, I saw that that spark between them is everything—it's much stronger than words, than anything, and its about the precious... how they heal each other through the story and the music. She's catatonic, she can only speak through her music and he reaches her.

AH: He wants to rescue her from *her* island. She is so clearly on her own desert island. To be thought of as psychotic is to be shipwrecked.

JT: Yes, exactly. So, the purpose of him telling it, the talent show, is just a ruse. It's really to rescue her because he loves her and their love is so precious in these desolate, desolate circumstances they live in, their ruined lives, like a shipwreck, that they rescue each other. She rescues him with her music and he rescues her with the story. As a writer I'm the first to say this, beyond all the words is the fragility and preciousness of their love for each other at the end—that's what it's all about. Going back to that old acting rule of what do you need to get, what's driving the scene. Then having Kristen, I started giving her lines to sing and then

I brought in the waltz. I said they have to dance. And Maria was wonderfully open and generous to these kinds of things—the writing became part of the production, and I gave Ciel more and more lines, until I think she now has six. Maria told me that Strauss didn't really like his music particularly for this, he wasn't very proud of it: he thought it was a bit of a sell-out musically. So I said to Kristin—can you play a song that he wrote that you think is really good? So Kristin knows it all, she's graduated from a music program at U of T, and she played "Morgen"—you know the one she sings in the middle—and I just melted.

AH: Every time she sang I was transported.

JT: Me too.

AH: And I think it was—aside from her voice, which is exquisite, and so pure—to some extent because she is so silent that when she does sing...

JT: ...it's glorious, it's that contrast.

AH: And she has very much a period look—the fragility, like a piece of porcelain. I'm interested too in how it ended up at The Theatre Centre.

JT: That is interesting. Franco Boni saw it in Summerworks[6] and expressed a real interest in it being at The Theatre Centre, so Maria and I talked and we thought well, we could push harder for Richard Rose, or CanStage or something. It got good reviews already, we knew it was successful. On the other hand, look where it is. In Parkdale, it's perfect for the piece. I was kind of feeling like at my age—I just turned 50—I should go back to my roots of poor theatre. To not be so cushioned by subscription, and take a chance. I don't know about that now, but that's what I felt. And Franco had generously offered us this chance and so we thought yeah, let's go with him. I will say also that nobody was jumping up to take it. I think they might have but they weren't. So we said "we're not even going to try, we're going to go with Franco."

AH: The space was perfect for it—right back to the bare brick walls, very simple stage design and yet it absolutely said everything that needed to be said. You really believed you were in Parkdale in one of those terrible church hall basements.

JT: In terms of audience, though, it was a really rude awakening for me. It made me realize, if I'm ever doing something like that again, before anything else, I'm getting a marketing person or publicist. Before you pay for a set or anything, because if you don't have people watching it, you don't got nothin'. Subscription is necessary, you can scoff at it as much as you like. Once we got stellar reviews, yes we got the nice houses. It filled up completely. Best reviews I've got in years, since *Lynndie England*, actually. If I'd got some of the reviews I'd had recently, we'd have got nobody at all! So now I know what it's like to be an American, to be totally dependent on reviews, where the critics are gods. I used to just scoff at reviews because it didn't matter, because I had my fan base, plus Tarragon's subscription, so combined we never suffered for audience. It's just a little annoying to be mocked and slagged in the newspaper, nobody likes it, but I didn't really care. It was very good to understand what people go through, young playwrights who are unknown, and yet still struggle to make theatre independently—I have such enormous admiration for them.

(2006)

Notes

[1] I would like to thank my daughter Erin MacKeen for her assistance in transcribing this interview.

[2] Judith Thompson's first adaptation of *Hedda Gabler* was commissioned by the Shaw Festival and first produced there at the Court House Theatre 30 July-2 September, 1991, directed by Judith Thompson, with Jim Mezon as Lövborg and Fiona Reid as Hedda. Ann Holloway played the role of Bertha.

[3] Yanna McIntosh played the title role in the first production of Judith Thompson's second adaptation of *Hedda Gabler*, produced by Volcano Theatre in association with Buddies in Bad Times Theatre, where it was performed 20 May-5 June 2005, directed by Ross Manson.

[4] *My Pyramids, or How I Got Fired From The Dairy Queen and Ended Up at Abu Ghraib, by Pvt. Lynndie England* was first produced in Toronto by Volcano Theatre at Factory Theatre's Studio Theatre on 1 November 2004, and again on 28 February 2005, directed by Ross Manson and performed by Waneta Storms. It was subsequently performed at the Traverse Theatre as part of the Edinburgh Fringe Festival in 2005.

[5] *Enoch Arden, by Alfred Lord Jabber and His Catatonic Songstress* was first produced at the Summerworks Festival in Toronto on August 5th, 7th, 11th, 12th, 13th and 14th, 2004 at Theatre Passe Muraille, and subsequently by The Theatre Centre, Toronto, 21 September-9 October 2005. Both productions were directed by Maria Lamont with John Fitzgerald Jay as Jabber and Kristen Mueller as Ciel.

[6] See note 5.

Work Cited

Masson, Jeffrey. *Assault on Truth: Freud's Suppression of the Seduction Theory*. New York: Farrar, Strauss, and Giroux, 1983.

Notes on Contributors

Jen Fletcher. During her graduate studies at the University of Guelph, Jennifer Lind Fletcher worked as a script assistant for the public workshop and premier production of Judith Thompson's *Sled*. After completing her MA, Jennifer helped to establish the University of Alberta Theatre Archives. Currently she serves as a Board Director for the Town Hall 1873: Port Perry Centre for the Performing Arts, and enjoys teaching high school students in Drama, Musical Theatre and English.

Ann Holloway is a professional actor and playwright living in Toronto. She acted in Judith Thompson's television movie, "Turning to Stone" in 1985, in the premiere of *Lion in the Streets* in 1990, and in Thompson's adaptation of *Hedda Gabler* for the Shaw Festival in 1991. She has most recently appeared in her own one-woman show *Kingstonia Dialect Perverso* and R.M. Vaughan's *Monster Trilogy*, both produced by Toronto's Buddies in Bad Times Theatre, and in the hit comedy television series "This Is Wonderland," for which she was nominated for a Gemini award. She is currently a Doctoral candidate at the Graduate Centre for the Study of Drama at the University of Toronto.

Nigel Hunt is a producer with CBC Newsworld and an independent writer/director. He used to edit a national theatre magazine and write regularly about theatre for various publications. He has an MA from the University of Toronto's Graduate Centre for the Study of Drama.

Ric Knowles is Professor of Theatre Studies at the University of Guelph, editor of *Canadian Theatre Review*, former editor-in-chief of *Modern Drama* (from 1999-2005), and general editor of the *Critical Perspectives on Canadian Theatre in English* series published by Playwrights Canada Press. He is the author of *The Theatre of Form and the Production of Meaning* (ECW 1999), *Shakespeare and Canada* (Lang 2004), and *Reading the Material Theatre* (Cambridge UP 2004); co-author of *Remembering Women Murdered by Men: Memorials Across Canada* (with the Cultural Memory Group, Sumach, 2006); editor of *Theatre in Atlantic Canada* (Mount Allison 1988) and *Judith Thompson* (Playwrights Canada 2005); and co-editor of *Modern Drama: Defining the Field* (with Joanne Tompkins and W. B. Worthen, University of Toronto Press 2003) and *Staging Coyote's Dream: An Anthology of First Nations Drama in English* (with Monique Mojica, Playwrights Canada, 2003). In 1990 he worked as assistant director and dramaturg on the premiere production of Judith Thompson's *Lion in the Streets* at the DuMaurier World Stage Festival.

Dean Palmer is a fine art photographer living and working in Guelph, Ontario. He has made a personal study of the medium of photography for the past 25 years. Dean credits his strong compositional and technical skills, and his attention to detail to studies in theatre and history at the University of Guelph. His passion is for location portraiture, and his work has been favourably compared to that of Walker Evans and August Sander. His award-winning images display a subtle richness and texture seldom seen in contemporary photography, and in 1997 he founded his own studio in downtown Guelph. The studio, *Dean Palmer Photography,* specializes in commercial, corporate, editorial and portrait photography and serves a wide-range of local, national and international clients.

Soraya Mariam Peerbaye is a writer living in Toronto. Her solo performance *GirlWrecked,* devised with director Karin Randoja, was produced in Toronto in 2001, and toured to local Toronto schools and the Artwallah Festival of South Asian arts in Los Angeles. She has served as Associate Artist with Nightwood Theatre, and playwright in residence with Theatre Direct.

Robyn Read is a graduate of the MA English program at the University of Guelph, where she wrote and directed several one act plays for student festivals and was a contributor to *The Orlando Project,* an online literary history of women's writing in the British Isles (forthcoming Spring 2006). Her creative writing has appeared in *Echolocation* and *Carousel,* and her work on Judith Thompson's *Capture Me* was published in *Theatre Research in Canada* and *Judith Thompson* (Spring 2005). As a consultant for the World University Service of Canada, she wrote profiles of past participants of the Student Refugee Program. Currently she is a PhD student in the Department of English at the University of Calgary.

Developmental dramaturg **Judith Rudakoff** (BA McGill, MA University of Alberta, PhD University of Toronto) has worked with emerging and established performing artists throughout Canada (from Nunavut to Yukon, from British Columbia to Prince Edward Island and points in between) and in Cuba, Denmark, South Africa, England and USA. Books include *Between the Lines: The Process of Dramaturgy* (Playwrights Canada, 2002, co-editor Lynn M. Thompson); *Fair Play: Conversations with Canadian Women Playwrights* (Simon & Pierre, 1989, co-editor Rita Much) and *Questionable Activities: Canadian Theatre Artists in Conversation with Canadian Theatre Students* (Playwrights Canada, 2000). Her articles have appeared in *The Drama Review, TheatreForum,* and *Canadian Theatre Review.* She is the creator of Elemental Lomograms, a transcultural methodology for initiating performance and visual art, a process which applies The Four Elements and incorporates her LOMO photography. She was the first Canadian honoured with the Elliott Hayes Prize in Dramaturgy for her work on South Asian choreographer Lata Pada's multidisciplinary work, *Revealed by Fire.* Rudakoff is a member of Playwrights Guild of Canada and Literary Managers and Dramaturgs of the Americas. She is a Professor of Theatre at Toronto's York University.

Sandra Tomc is a writer, screenwriter, and associate professor of English at the University of British Columbia. Apart from her film and television work with her husband, Roger Larry ("Tested," "Knockin' on Heaven's Door," and "Crossing"), Sandra is working on her next screenplay, "Pippa's Dream", for which she recently received funding from Telefilm Canada. Sandra's scholarly work, for which she has received a number of awards, focuses on American literature and contemporary theatre and popular culture. Her essays have been published in *The Cambridge Companion to Edgar Allan Poe*, *American Quarterly* and *Representations*. Sandra is currently finishing a book on nineteenth-century American magazine writers and their relationship to leisure. She lives in Vancouver with Roger and their daughter, Scarlett.

Andrew Vowles is a writer in the Office of Communications and Public Affairs at the University of Guelph. Now living in Hamilton, he has been writing for 20 years, after having completed an undergrad degree in biology at U of G.

Eleanor Wachtel is the host of CBC Radio's "Writers & Company" and "The Arts Tonight". Her three books of interviews are *Original Minds* (Harper Collins), *More Writers & Company* and *Writers & Company* (both Knopf Canada).

Cynthia Zimmerman has been a commentator on Canadian playwriting and on the voice of women on the Canadian stage for her whole career at Glendon College, York University, where she is a Professor in the English department. Previously book review editor of the international journal *Modern Drama* and currently a member of its Advisory Board, Zimmerman has authored or co-authored several books, including *Playwriting Women: Female Voices in English Canada*, and produced numerous articles, chapters, and public papers. She also edited the successful anthology, *Taking the Stage* for Playwrights Canada Press. Pleased to have edited the first volume of *Sharon Pollock: Collected Works*, also for Playwrights Canada, she is currently working on the subsequent volumes as well as books on B.C. playwright Betty Lambert and Ontario playwright Carol Bolt.